MW01690475

Get Out of Your Mind!

7 steps to creating long-term success & life-long fulfilment

Adila Vahed

Acknowledgements

With happiness and gratitude, I acknowledge:

My Infinite Creator - He is the Lord of the Worlds, the most Beneficent and the most Merciful. As the Divine Intelligence, He is all knowing, all forgiving and the source of peace and safety. As a majestic giver of blessings, the giver of honour, He is omnipotent and just. He is the wise, glorious giver of life and guardian.

My dearest mother and father, Razia Bibi and Yunus Goolam Hoosen Vahed, who have been my support structure throughout my life - they are my biggest fans and critics! I express sincere gratitude for the encouragement, values and morals that you both have instilled in me all the days of my life.

Muhammad Ra'id, my best friend, pillar of strength and source of unconditional support and encouragement. Thank you for holding my hand from darkness through to the light.

My grandfather. Hajee Suleman Ismail, who has been my mentor in more ways than one. Your wisdom, experience and way of life have taught me much more than any book I have ever read in my life.

My three sisters and all of my family for their patience, love and support through each step of my life

Catherine Jenkin, my editor. Thank you for your time, awesome support and faith in me.

Raymond Aaron & Jennifer Le, for bringing this wonderful opportunity into my life

And a special thank you to each and every person that I have met over the past 27 years of my life who have contributed towards my growth in some way or the other. Meeting each of you has had a profound, direct effect on my life journey. You have set alight my passion and honed my inspiration

Foreword by Raymond Aaron

"Get out of your Mind!" by Adila Vahed invites you to find your spark of inspiration through her 7 step guide to creating long-term success and life-long filfullment. This young entrepeneur's creativity and straight forward approach allows you to resonate with hard hitting challenges that you may experience in your daily life and harnessing the ability to overcome them.

This book engages readers across all spheres of life providing insight and understanding as to how one can change their mind-set and create a reality of success and happiness.

Adila outlines several aspects of life from finance, health, relationships to finding one's true purpose and ways in which you are able to take control of your mind by understanding how it works.

She also embraces and accurately explains the power of the sub conscious mind as well as the existence of the ego throughout the flow of this book.

Adila offers self-help exercises toward the end of her book which are valuable and constructive towards one's own personal growth and development.

At a young age of 27, Adila's experiences and constant research in pursuit of self-acceptance and search for a better understanding of her true purpose in life has brought her to this moment.

In this book you will explore the ego and true self and the realms of existence. This will allow you to gain a better understanding of your purpose and assist you to work towards your vision using your goals as your benchmark!

Raymond Aaron

Author of "Double your income doing what you Love"

New York Times 10 Bestselling Author

Preface

For far too long, I remained in a state of unconsciousness. For everything that went wrong in my life, I always found someone or something else to blame. I consistently blamed external forces, circumstances and situations for things that happened to me.

But, from young, I had dreams. I'd daydream of a life filled with love, perfection and no difficulties. Yet, every time an obstacle appeared, I'd let go of one of those beautiful dreams. As a result, many years passed where I'd let go of a dream and watch it be replaced by a difficulty.

Complaining used to be part of my daily prayer. Somehow, it seems that if you talk about your problems, you feel better. It is only years later that I have begun to understand the consequences of complaint and how complaining does not positively serve my life, my unique reality or me.

Just when I thought that there was no hope for my future, something inside of me was born. It was my first spark of inspiration. The voice inside me started saying something very different - something much better than before. I no longer felt like a victim. I no longer felt sorry for myself.

All thoughts of hopelessness left my body and mind almost like a miracle. It was, however, neither a miracle nor a stroke of good luck. It was the transformation from unconsciousness to consciousness, a breathtakingly brilliant awakening into a new realm of existence.

I felt as if I had been given a brand new mind. A few years ago, I called it amazing. Today, I call it enlightenment like a breath of fresh air. The day I woke up from the deep sleep within the spheres of my mind, I realised that I had finally taken control of my mind.

Every single person that you will meet through this journey of your life is no coincidence. Every illness or heartbreak you are ever faced with is never a stroke of bad luck. Each and every experience is something unique and in fact is part of the reality that you have created with your own two hands.

So whoever you are and wherever you are right now, your change begins this very moment.

This book is not about my life story or me. This book is about you. Take control and get out of your mind!

With Love and Light,

Adila

Contents

Chapter One

Gratitude

"A thankful person is thankful under all circumstances"

Baha'u'llah (1817 – 1892)

Successful Leader Interview

Mr Yacoob Moosa

CEO, Bargain Wholesalers, Port Shepstone, KZN, South Africa

Tell us a little more about your humble beginnings?

My grandfather, Mahomed Moosa, came from India in the 1940's in search of opportunity. He found employment as a salesman in a retail store in Ixopo while my dad, Ismail Moosa, schooled at a local Zulu-medium school where he leant to speak Zulu "like a Zulu".

After a few years my grandfather was transferred to Port Shepstone. After some years of saving, the family started a little grocery retail store, Bargain Bazaar, in Port Shepstone in the 1950's. Soon opportunity emerged to open a "Holiday Makers' Shop" catering for holidaymakers from the then-Transvaal.

With hard work and a fine understanding of the Zulu language, Dad, with the support of his brothers, was able to develop relationships with local Black traders and the idea of "grocery wholesaling was borne". Under Apartheid law it was difficult securing warehousing space in town, so, in 1973, Bargain Wholesalers was formally established in Marburg, on the outskirts of town. Through God's Grace business went well resulting in establishing more branches in rural areas. Today, the family is grateful to have ten grocery wholesale and retail outlets severing the lower south Coast of KZN and Eastern Cape employing about a 1000 staff. During the course of the years, dad's brothers diversified into Oil and Soap Manufacturing (Sanola Oil Mills) and sweet manufacturing (Marburg Sweets). The family business initiative is hence in the 4th generation since the arrival of my grandfather on the South African shores

What is your definition of success?

People are prone to defining success only in financial terms. Whilst money is an integral part of everyday life, one's success (and happiness) is determined by how well connected one is with God and with one's fellow men. This requires cultivating a pure heart and a generous spirit

What makes you a leader?

There is a lot of literature available to answer that question. Taking responsibility to help improve things wisely makes anyone a leader.

What advice do you have to offer young aspiring entrepreneurs?

Develop a strong yearning to succeed, work hard, plan well, play fair and trust in God.

What kind of mind-set do you have? Tell us a little more about your thoughts and how they affect your life?

Bargain Wholesalers' success comes from dad's mind-set. Dad's mind-set focused on four principles: work passionately; be firm but fair; lead by example and leave work at work and, why do tomorrow what you can do today?

Gratitude for Life

Appreciation for your blessings

It has taken me nine years of my life to meet you at this point. I am here, and you are reading this, for a purpose. I am here because you have summoned me into your existence. There is something inside of you that made a serious decision to want something different, to want different results in your life. So embrace this moment, turn each new page of this book as if you were creating a whole new reality for yourself and usher in a new inner and outer world of change.

The only reason that you do not have what you want right now in your life is simple. You have not yet expressed enough gratitude for that which you were already blessed with. From the day you were born up until the day you were able to earn an income, you were taken care of by your parents and life itself. Thereafter, you found a job and started taking care of yourself. Well, at least this is what you are led to believe. You were born trusting the processes of life and it has brought you to this point in your life. The question then arises; have you been grateful for it all? And what is your definition of gratitude?

To me, gratitude is the memory of the heart. It is having the ability to wake up each morning with realisation and deep thanks for what you have been blessed with. Each one of us has the habit of complaint. There seems to always be something to be unhappy about or someone who has upset us. I have learnt that complaint is poverty and gratitude is riches. Accept things for what they are, and rejoice in the fact that you have experienced them to learn something. It is only from this point on that you will receive what you want.

Until recently, I had been the perfect example of an ungrateful person. Nothing had ever been good enough for me. I somehow managed to find problems in most of my life situations - my relationship, my work, my health and my finances. It seemed that nothing was ever good enough to keep me happy! If I had a desire for something, I complained because I didn't have it. When I did eventually receive it, it didn't matter anymore because I now had a new desire that needed fulfilling. The vicious cycle continued for years, until I actually began losing the things that I did have.

Until, one day, I awoke to the realisation that I had been in some deep, unconscious sleep. I cannot remember how it happened exactly – either I had read something, or someone had said something to get me out of that slumber. But awaken I did! I decided to put pen to paper and make a list of all that I had. Even before that list was completed, I had run out of paper and another realisation dawned on me. I had more than enough, too much really – much more than many others! I realised that what I didn't have, was sincere appreciation for all that I did have - and due to lack of appreciation, complaining seemed to have been the best thing to do at the time. With this realisation, came the change. And let me say this to you, if this change does not come from a deep sense of self and from a desire within you, you will not really change. If you do not sincerely believe that a change needs to take place in your inner world, do not expect your outer world to be any different from what it is right now.

I was recently in a very interesting discussion with a relative, and we spoke about realistic ways to make a difference in the lives of others. What can one possibly do to let others know that they are not victims and that they should take responsibility for their own lives? I went on to speak about gratitude and how it can change a person's life. She then said to me "Adila, if a person is poor and has no food to eat and goes to bed hungry, and then you come along and tell them to be grateful, do you think that they are going to listen to you and be grateful when their tummy is hungry? They will not be thinking about being grateful or thinking positive, they will be thinking about how to get food to satisfy their hunger".

That kind of approach is self-sabotage. I am saying to you that you cannot receive anything in your life until you become grateful for what you have. So, whilst you are thinking of food and focusing on your hunger, you are depriving yourself even more by not wanting to be thankful for being alive. There is always something to be grateful for no matter how bad the situation is. Our minds deceive us into believing that everything is always wrong and nothing is going right. Therefore, as long as we focus on the problems before us, so we will garner and discover more problems.

If a hungry person chooses to not be grateful for life and he focuses and thinks about his hunger, does that mean that the next day his hunger will be satisfied? If he cannot physically, externally do something about his hunger, he is left with the ability to think. If he can think, then perhaps he should consider thoughts of appreciation. God is aware of everything. There is nothing and nobody in any corner of this world that God does not know about - whether he is suffering or enjoying life. And there is no creation on Earth or in the Universe that is not aware of God and His Infinite Divine Intelligence, as He exists within his creation. The lesson here is - no matter how bad the situation may seem, if you cannot think of being grateful, at least think of God. That alone is appreciation. In the remembrance of God, battered hearts find rest. There will be food for this man. There is abundance in the Universe for every creation that exists. If you do not want something, why would it come to you? If you are not appreciative of what you are and what you have, of what use will more of anything be to you?

The first step to being grateful is to make a list of everything that you already have. This can and should include your job, education, food, shelter, clothing, electricity, your spouse, religion, parents, family, children, siblings, health, car, your five senses that allow you to see, smell, hear, taste and feel…the list can seem infinite when you start to write it all down. Begin with identifying everything that you do have that you need to be grateful for and then be truly grateful for it. How? By feeling grateful. The appreciation that you think and feel needs to flow through each cell within your body. You first need to make a decision about your thoughts and channel your thoughts towards gratitude. These thoughts will be followed by a belief that you are indeed a grateful person. Soon afterwards, you will begin to feel grateful because your thought, belief and emotion will lead to actions and the behaviour of a grateful person.

Changing your reality

No matter who you are, what you do, or what circumstances your life includes, you can transform your reality. Being grateful will change your entire life. Analyse the current situation of your life in all areas, including those of finance, health, relationships, career and home. If you identify which area of life is lacking and requires change, it is that specific area that actually requires more appreciation. This may sound contradictory, but remember that God's Treasury has more than enough for everyone. By saying you are lacking, it implies there is not enough in God's Treasury and in this statement there lies ingratitude. Therefore, by being grateful, you are saying that you truly believe in God's Power to provide you with more.

Each area of your life contributes to your success and your desire for inner peace. If your relationship is not fulfilling, you will experience emotional turmoil and unhappiness. If you do not have enough money to pay the bills, you will experience stress and tension. If your health is deteriorating, you will lack concentration and energy. If you dislike your job, you will wake up feeling burdened, feel demotivated and you will go to bed with a restless mind. If you make a conscious decision, however, to change the very situation that perplexes you, you will think and act very differently

3 Simple steps to changing the basic thought processes of complaint into appreciation:

- When you wake up each morning, bless the morning light and give thanks for being alive to see another day.
- Each step you take should be filled with thankfulness, from the time you put on your shoes, through your morning ablutions, eating breakfast and en route to work.
- Repeat the words "Thank you, thank you, thank you" as you identify your blessings.

When something inside of you gives you a clear indication that there is more to life than your daily complaint, then only will you realise the value of what you have. So, in order to change your reality, you must begin by identifying all things that you are grateful for first.

I remember being ungrateful some years ago because I had to wake up each morning, make my way to a colleague's house and go to work through a lift club they operated. I complained because I had to wake up a few hours earlier in order to get to her house so that I could be on time for work. I complained because I didn't have my own car to drive myself to work. I complained because work was a quite a distance away from home. A few weeks later, my colleague informed me that she is unable to assist me with transport any longer because she has found another job in a different area. Not only did this devastate me but I also complained that I would now have to commute via public transport. No sooner did I realise that I did not want that, and then I made a conscious decision to become grateful. So from the very next day, I woke up each morning with gratitude. I was grateful for the fact that I was alive, that I had the perfect gift of health which allowed me to go to work, I was grateful that I had a job to begin with and I was sincerely grateful that I had transport every day to get to work. I changed my attitude. I began embracing that which I complained about. I started being grateful for my colleague, her car, her fuel, her time and effort in assisting me and most of all, I was grateful that even though I did not have my own car, I had transport and that was more than enough to be grateful for.

Within two months of this change in thought and belief, I bought my very first car and found a job closer to home. A miracle? Magic you say? No, it most certainly was not. It was just a sincere appreciation for what I had been blessed with. When you become a grateful person, you will find a flow of abundance into your life. Being ungrateful only leads to more being taken away from your life.

Abundance can and will only flow into your life once you express gratefulness and rejoice in your blessings. God loves each and every one of us and He wills abundance for us in our lives. We are the ones who create a life of lack and loss through our thoughts and actions when we are ungrateful.

Gratitude for my Income

Do you work in a job that leaves you dissatisfied? Do you find yourself waking up each morning, with a sense of irritation and foreboding clouding your perspective for the day ahead? The thought of the same routine, office, demanding boss and irritating colleagues fills you with dread, and the notions of office gossip and not having enough time for yourself, weigh you down.

All of this, coupled with a salary that seems insufficient, leads you to compare your life with others and you're left feeling ungrateful. You may even consider yourself a victim of a system you have no control over. At some point, your negative thoughts will reflect in your actions, and you'll end up being unproductive and disillusioned.

That's why it's vital to remember that whatever you think about, you bring about. Perhaps it is time to realise that you will no longer play the game of blame and look for anything outside of you to be the cause of your circumstance? The answer is simple. You lack gratitude. Something has got to give.

What will you do to change the current situation? Remember – I said it earlier - every situation can and will change if you want it to be different from what it is right now. The reason that you are going through all of this misery and anxiety in your work is because you are not expressing gratitude for your job and its blessings. Try to be grateful, even for the things and people that you dislike. Your entire situation will begin to change when you replace complaint with appreciation.

Begin by appreciating the fact that you have a job. If you do not have a job, then start appreciating the job that is still to come and the journey you are experiencing in your search for it. Be thankful for it in advance and summon it into your existence. Be grateful for the opportunities to search for a job, the interviews you may undergo and remember that God knows what you want, before you even ask. The right things for you are already out there, waiting for you. All you have to do is be grateful for what you have, be sure of what you want, and ask.

Many people have worked in the same job for most of their lives. You'll meet them and they'll immediately tell you how they dislike their job and are currently seeking alternative employment. Yet, a decade later, they are still in the same position, with the same company and will still tell you that they're looking to change jobs because they're unhappy.

Later in life, you will find that this very same person in fact worked in that position for that company all their life through to retirement. There was never improvement in position or salary let alone a change in employment. Why do you think this was the case?

That's simple. To a degree, that person was grateful for their job because had they not expressed gratitude, they would have become jobless within a few months of their job. So this is a positive action. Appreciation is important.

If, however, you took a closer look at their thought patterns, you'd discover that they harboured and expressed complaints throughout their life. They have continuously complained about how they were unhappy in that position and company and always talked about finding a new job. How is it ever possible to attain anything more than what you currently have right now in your life if you are complaining? It is not possible. The anchor of complaints that they rested their life on has never permitted them to strive towards anything better or more rewarding. If you look around you, you will find many people that have much less than you and that alone, is a valid reason for you to express gratitude for what you have been blessed with.

It is very easy for me to declare that I am a grateful person. Gratitude is a virtue however it is not something that you begin and once you get what you want, then you stop. Gratitude does not work that way. Gratitude is a state of mind, a constant path and it has to be instilled into your memory as part of your everyday existence. It will become part of your identity, something embedded into your very existence and the inner realm of your consciousness.

The second step is to be grateful for the people you most dislike, and this can be difficult! It is through them that you have the opportunity to strengthen yourself, to grow and to develop into a more conscious being. Start being grateful for these people around you. Stop complaining about them and start looking for things within them that are of good quality and character. If you look deep enough, surely you will find good.

Whatever you identify in another person already exists within you, for what you see in someone else is just yourself reflecting back.

I would like to go into more detail here. I do not believe that there is any person that you will meet in your life as a result of coincidence. God has created the Universe and mankind in such a way that it has been planned with surgical precision. Every person that you have met or will ever come to meet will have a true meaning and purpose behind it. Of course, not every person you meet will necessary be your best friend or someone that you can trust but they will serve a purpose.

All of us have, at some point in our life, been hurt by someone else's actions. You would have experienced some sort of pain, disappointment, anger, resentment and heartbreak due to someone who did not meet your expectations. The first reaction to pain and disappointment is resentment and hard heartedness. You close off a certain part of your emotional self where you no longer care for the person who has hurt you. And if you do care, you will never dare to show it to them or anyone else for that matter. You must remember something very important.

Since there is no such thing as coincidence, you will come to understand that if someone has hurt you, it was his or her purpose in your life. You cannot tell me that if you were hurt, there was no lesson to be learnt. Every situation that life presents to you - whether it is good or bad - is in your life for a specific reason and most of the time, it is for you to learn something valuable and become a stronger human being. It is only when you experience disappointment and pain, are you able to depend on your own strength and become wiser.

So in essence, should you not express gratitude for all people that have been and will enter your life? There is no single person you should be ungrateful for, no matter how he or she hurt you or what resentment you hold towards him or her. When you learn to truly, sincerely express gratitude for that person, you will soon realise that the pain and resentment no longer dwells within your heart.

The third step is to be appreciative of the salary that you earn. As you spend each cent, write the expense on paper and next to it, a note of gratitude for the bill and the money you have to pay for it. Embrace your expenses and at the same time, embrace the money that you earn. Do not worry yourself with how much the person next to you earns and spends. Do not compare your life to his. Concern yourself with only yourself. Be happy with what you earn and most importantly - express sincere gratitude for your money, your job, your colleagues, your challenges and your superiors.

Money is a sensitive topic for most people. People react differently when it comes to thoughts and beliefs about money, as some see it as a wonderful thing to own, and others may see it as a curse. The very same thought goes into receiving bills. Why would you want to complain about receiving a bill when you created that bill to begin with? And how was it ever possible for you to create that bill? You had to spend money or be credit worthy to the bank. In order for you to credit worthy, you must have proof of income. Is it possible to receive a bill if you have not proved that you earn an income? And if you earn an income, isn't that just an amazing thing to be grateful for? You have a job and earn an income in a world beleaguered by job losses and terrible economic loss.

From today, I ask you to welcome your bills into your life. Let it be something that you look forward to receiving and paying. Receive your bills with a smile and sincerely feel grateful for it. When it is time to make payment, do it with a smile and feel good about making that payment. That is gratitude. Soon, you will notice that you will receive more bills in your life and the best part is you will also receive sufficient money to be able to pay for those bills. This is not magic. This is appreciation. God will continue to bless each one of us in our lives where we are appreciative.

Each one of us goes through a difficult experience in our lives. If life went swimmingly all along, worked out perfectly and you were to write out a list of everything that you are grateful for, it would be very easy to do. Your list would be long as you wrote down all of the wonderful things that are happening.

The best time, however, for gratitude is when you are experiencing a challenge, a difficulty, a lack or a loss of something that you hold value for. This is the true test of your gratitude. This is when you need to be most appreciative for everything in your life including the pain. The situation is in your life for a reason. It is there to strengthen you and assist you towards delving deeper into yourself and learning things about yourself that you did not know before. There cannot be pleasure without pain. There cannot be support without challenges; there cannot be success without failure. So when you are faced with a difficult situation in any area of your life, choose to be grateful rather than complain about it. When you are aware that complaining will not improve the situation in anyway, it will be easier to become grateful, no matter how severe the situation may be. You will begin to understand that gratitude enhances the quality of your life.

We are so captivated by thoughts of the past and the future that we forget to live in the present moment. We forget about what is actually happening right now in our lives. We are so distracted by what is still going to happen that we become filled with worry, anxiety and complaint.

Today, this present moment was your "future" in the past, was it not? So you are living in your future, if that makes sense. The past is over and done with which means that you cannot go back to it. You can think about it but you cannot physically go back into the past. And the same can be said for the future, for we have yet to discover the secrets of time travel and you cannot skip ahead and change the future.

So why is it necessary to think about or worry about what is still to happen in the future when you are in the present moment? Unless you have some sort of guarantee that you will live for the next 10 or 20 years? The only guarantee you have in life is the present moment. And it is through the present moment that you create your future.

You create it with thoughts, words or beliefs of complaint or of gratitude. Whichever of the two you choose, will determine the quality of the life you will live. It is important to not resist the present moment but live in it. So if something happens right now and it does not meet your approval, accept it as the disguise or form it takes in the present moment.

If you are finding it difficult to begin this process, make a decision to temporarily take all of your current problems and put them into a box. Decide now that you will put each difficulty, challenge and circumstance that you perceive as a problem and store it away into this mental box. Once you have done that, you no longer have any of these to face at the moment. You can now concentrate on being thankful for everything that you have by opening up your very own gratitude journal. Be sure to consistently, every day; express your gratitude for your blessings. Below is a basic idea that you can follow for your gratitude journal:

17th October 2013

Dear God, Universe, Infinite Intelligence, thank you for my life, my breath and my beautiful health which keeps me alive, Thank you.

Dear God, Universe, Infinite Intelligence, thank you for my home, the food that I eat daily, this shelter that you provide, clothing, electricity and water, Thank you.

Dear God, Universe, Infinite Intelligence, thank you for my parents, spouse, children, siblings and their well-being, their perfect health, their education and their provisions that you ordain, Thank you.

Dear God, Universe, Infinite Intelligence, thank you for my job which brings me this salary and allows me to pay my bills each month and provides me with comfort and allows me to take care of myself and help others, Thank you.

Your gratitude journal can be more defined where you specifically are thankful for people by name or you may wish to write down each area of your life in more detail with more information. Your gratitude journal is yours to create, define and fill – the only rule for it is that you say “Thank you” every day.

Remember not only are you expressing gratitude to God but you are also embedding gratitude into your spirit, body, mind and life.

After thirty days of dedicatedly expressing your gratitude through your gratitude journal, it's time to take your problems out of that box you created in your mind. Open the box and begin to go through your problems that you put into that box. You will be pleasantly surprised to find that the box will be empty. And if for some reason, you open that box and you still find problems in it, then you need to continue expressing gratitude for your blessings. At some point - and I assure you of this - you will open the box and it will be empty.

You will search deep within it convincing yourself that you had several problems, challenges and difficulties and you are certain that you kept them safe in that box however you will be pleasantly surprised when you cannot find it any longer. This is the power of gratitude.

God is Great and He will remove your challenges from your path. That is His doing. It is not your duty to remove your challenges. It is not your responsibility to think about your problems and dwell on them. It is not your duty to search for solutions. It is, however, your duty to be sincerely and completely grateful for your blessings. God will take care of the rest on your behalf, as He has the power and the Infinite Intelligence. Your job is to focus on the good and wonderful things that life gives you.

You have in your hands the building blocks for the foundation of your inner and outer world. If you want an amazing life, the key is to be grateful for that which you have been blessed with. The foundation of your life is based on how appreciative you have been and will continue to be. As each block begets more blocks, your life will become filled with abundance, inner peace and contentment.

Make all your dreams a reality

We've all said it: "I want wealth. I want success. I want..." There is abundance in the Universe for each one of us. There is no divine decision taken where God apportions wealth to one person, and poverty to another. The biggest mistake we can make is to play the "blame game". We blame God, we blame people and we blame circumstances for everything that we feel we lack. The day you look within will be the very day you find the answers to every question you have.

Dreaming is part of who we are. We dream of a life filled with abundance, happiness, wealth and success. Many of us even aspire towards opening and building a profitable business, where we hire staff, create products we believe in and attract clients who will bring us money.

You cannot get all of this in life if you don't really want it. Nor will you attain it by comparing your life with others and feeling like a victim of circumstance as a result. A negative mind-set manifests a negative reality for you, and the act of complaining creates negativity.

Gratitude, however, enables positive change to manifest in your life.

It is time for a change. Now that you understand the power of gratitude and the wealth that lies within, you can make life-transforming decisions. For now, do not concentrate on the end result. Focus on the sincerity of your efforts and the results will follow.

We all want wealth and success but it is our choices that define our ability to attain them. We must choose wisely, sincerely express our gratitude and accept that – no matter what – we have a life of abundance. We must replace complaint with gratitude and remove all expectations from our mind-sets. We must trust the process of life and in the Almighty plan of God.

It's time to create your reality and that reality is now. You have no guarantees except this very moment so, put your problems in that box you've created, open your gratitude journal and begin your amazing journey.

Self Help & Assessment Exercises

Chapter One - Gratitude for Life

Points to Remember:

- Open a gratitude journal; this could be a regular hard cover book or a diary of your choice.
- Each day, write down the date and time at the top of your page before you begin writing

- To the best of your ability, make time to pen your thoughts at least once per day
- You may not always find time to write in your journal daily, however, like you eat everyday, no matter how busy you are; the same amount of effort should be put into being grateful and making note of that which you appreciate.
- Everything that you write, you must feel in your heart, you must believe as true and experience emotions of complete peace & appreciation as you write.

Self Help Exercise 1

- Write down at least 10 problems or challenges that you are currently experiencing in your life.

- From the above list of 10 challenges, select 3 of the most serious and worrying problems that you are faced with.

- Now, for each challenge, write down your thoughts, beliefs & emotions below:

1. **Challenge 1:**

Current Thoughts:

Current Beliefs:

Current Emotions:

- For each challenge you are faced with, write down at least 2 things from this challenge, that you can be grateful for;

Challenge 1

I am grateful
for/that_____________________________________

Below, write down 2 advantages that you are experiencing right now in your life as a result of each challenge

Challenge 1

Advantage 1

Advantage 2

For 4 weeks in a row, at least once a week, re-do the above exercise.

You may choose to change your top 10 and even your top 3 challenges per week.

Once you have reached week 4, make one list of all of your problems as well as all of blessings and benefits.

You will be pleasantly surprised to discover a much shorter list of problems and a longer list of blessings!

Self Help Exercise 2

45 day Complaint Detox

- Wake up each day and decide on a time of day where you will write in your journal
- Gratitude needs to become the memory of your heart
- Write down a minimum of 10 things that you are grateful for in your life. The list must include people or objects for example your parents, children, siblings, good health, education, car, fuel, cell phone, airtime, shelter, clothing, electricity, food and drink, your 5 senses, your job and your income. The list is endless and you can elaborate further. Each sentence should begin with "Dear God... followed by your thanks for the blessing and end with Thank you God for this blessing in my life for example: "Dear God, thank you for the food and water in my daily life, thank you for this blessing"

Gratitude List

1. ______________________________
2. ______________________________
3. ______________________________
4. ______________________________
5. ______________________________

- Once you have completed your list of things and people that you are grateful for, write down a minimum of 10 things that you want in your life. This could be anything from a better job, a higher salary, another child, your own home or better health. Decide on a minimum of 10 things that you want in your life that you believe will improve and enhance the quality of your life and your sentence could be written as follows "Dear God, I want to move into my own home soon"

<u>What I want List</u>

1. ____________________
2. ____________________
3. ____________________
4. ____________________
5. ____________________
6. ____________________
7. ____________________
8. ____________________
9. ____________________
10. ____________________

The immediate next step that follows that sentence is as follows "Dear God, thank you for my new home, it is really beautiful. I love the 2 bedrooms and spacious lounge area. This home you have blessed me with is lovely and is exactly how I imagined it to be. It feels really great to wake up in my new home every morning and it is a blessing to live here, Thank you, Thank you, Thank you" Be thankful for each of your above wants in advance as if it is already yours! Feel it, think it! Believe it! Now write down how grateful you are for it:

<u>Thanking in advance</u>

1. ______________________________
2. ______________________________
3. ______________________________
4. ______________________________
5. ______________________________

6. As you may have noticed, I have asked you to first make a list of everything that you are grateful for, moving onto listing everything that you want in your life and lastly, by feeling, believing and being grateful for what you want in advance as if it is already yours.

By doing this, you are expressing gratitude for that which is still to come into your life and you have attached sincere emotion and belief towards these wants and in good time, you will soon see things in your life changing for your benefit.

This must be done for 45 consecutive days in a row in order for you to embed gratitude in your mind, body and soul. Through that, it will become embedded into your very existence in this world. Soon, you will find situations in your life change dramatically and it is through faith and consistency that this will happen.

Chapter Two

A New Consciousness

"Infinite riches are all around you if you will open your mental eyes and behold the treasure house of infinity within you'

Joseph Murphy

Successful Leader Interview

Mr Shabir Chohan

CEO, Albaraka Bank, Durban, South Africa

Tell us a little about your beginnings?

I was born into a family that owned a business called Chohan's Spice. My father's business was the topic of discussion at the dinner table every evening and my life revolved around this family business. During school vacation, I spent my days working for the business. From a young age, being in grade 8, I had a keen interest in figures. I knew then that I wanted to be a Chartered Accountant. I read the financial mail often, followed the stock market and shares and was very passionate about finance. After matric, I went on to further my studies gaining a Bachelor of Commerce Degree at the Howard College Campus of the University of KwaZulu-Natal. I then completed a diploma in Accounting and finally completed by board exams at the age of 21 followed by qualifying as a Chartered

Accountant by the age of 24. I was first in class throughout University life. My career began with the accounting firm PWC and soon after, I moved to their London offices in 1990, and remained there until 1992. This was one of the best experiences of my life as I travelled extensively during my time at this office. I returned to South Africa & worked for the Banco Group of Companies and was appointed as financial manager for the Muslim Financial Indian Board. I was head hunted by Ithala and was finance executive at the age of 30. I joined Albaraka Bank in 2004 where I started as a specialised projects consultant and today I am the CEO of Albaraka Bank.

What is your definition of success?

I believe that focus and determination is the core focus of any individual. When you set your heart and your mind out to do something, you must be determined to follow your purpose, remained focus until it is achieved. Ultimate success is being able to maintain a balanced life. Also, it is important for one to have an ethical approach and stick to their values and etiquettes. Your values and etiquettes are your guidelines to make decisions around any matter concerned. Once a plan is set up, it needs to be strategically implemented in order for achievement to take place.

What makes you a leader?

Well, firstly, I am surrounded by a competent, hardworking and dedicated team. I am part of that team of about 300 people and I believe that it takes a team to produce results, as there is only a fair amount that can be done by one person. I introduce an element of innovation and creativity and others believe in my purpose and share in my vision. Everyone needs to be on bus, we can change positions whenever necessary but ultimately, we are all headed in the same direction and this is my approach as a leader. As a leader, communication is key. Talking to my team is important to me. I think that it is important for a leader to be on the ground and understand the operations of a business and be engaged. In this way, I am able to observe and provide input where necessary.

What advice do you have to offer to young aspiring entrepreneurs?

You must have a dream and that dream becomes your vision. Have a clear indication of your vision and pioneer towards achieving it. Today, the world is filled with brilliant people however the incorrect attitude. With the wrong attitude, success cannot happen. The degree of arrogance and need for instant gratification must cease to exist. It is not your aptitude; it is your attitude that will determine your altitude. Always pay interest in whatever you are doing. Remain focused. Instant gratification is a short-term approach and is not sustainable. Patience plays a very important role in achieving the desired success. Work towards your vision with determination and patience.

What kind of mind-set do you have? Tell us a little more about your thoughts and how they affect your life?

I confront all issues with a positive approach. No matter how negative a situation may be, I purely focus on solutions and outcome. I rid all negativity from my thought process and work towards changing the negative into a positive. I do not stress over things I have no control over, and focus my positive attention on that which I do have control over. I believe it is important for one to take responsibility for their thoughts. Your thoughts can influence your reality so be careful of what you think and if you are faced with a problem, think about the possible solutions and your role in creating that solution.

Clarity of the Two Minds

It's quite common to be in "two minds" about a decision. I've never really understood what that phrase meant – does it mean indecisive, confused or uncertain?

It was only in recent years that I came to completely grasp the concept of having two minds. The truth is there is only one mind but it has two spheres. These spheres are respectively known as the self-conscious and subconscious mind. Last year at a cancer support group where I spoke to thirty cancer patients and focused on practical strategies for them to imbue positivity into their lives, I was asked to explain my perspective on the two spheres of our minds.

Well you see, each one of us have this self-conscious mind and this is also known as the captain of the ship. The self-conscious mind is all about itself. It's all about you, your ego and the part of you that enjoys the material wealth that can be found in this world. This is the egocentric you, that gets caught up in "drama" and has the potential to be manipulative. The self-conscious mind takes very little notice of the world, as it consumed by millions of thoughts that enter it every day. Due to the fact that the self-conscious mind is controlling and self-centred, it is not aware at all times. It acts unconsciously. It believes the positive and the negative. There is always conflict in the self-conscious mind. There is always drama and chaos. The self-conscious mind is often filled with thoughts of the past and the future, and it very rarely lives in the present moment. When the self-conscious mind thinks, it lacks gratitude in its thinking and it focuses on complaints. Something is always going wrong. Nothing or nobody is ever good enough.

Emotions are attached to the self-conscious mind, including love, joy and pleasure. But, in the same way, sadness, pain and bitterness are also attached to the self-conscious mind. The ego lives within the self-conscious mind and feeds off thoughts about the past and future. The self-conscious mind wants to be the master, yet it submits to the ego, which immediately makes it self-defeating. So although this self-conscious mind is smart and intelligent and navigates the ship, it fails to realise that whatever it believes, will become a reality. I will explain further once we understand who the subconscious mind is.

The sub-conscious mind can be regarded as the humble, obedient servant. It is a state of mind that is pure and flawless. To me, the place where God exists within the human is the sub-conscious mind. The sub-conscious mind makes no judgement and no decisions. To the sub-conscious mind, everything is always perfect. There is always peace and serenity. There is permanent beauty in its existence. It is this part of our mind that cannot determine right from wrong or black from white, because whatever it is fed, it shall accept and manifest. The sub-conscious mind controls and governs the functions of our body and our organs. It serves its duty to the human by circulating our blood; digesting our food and ensuring our organs function accordingly.

The sub-conscious mind has healing power to resolve any illness or problem within the body. It is important for you to understand the interaction and the relationship between the self-conscious and sub-conscious mind. In order for your external conditions to improve, you must work on the internal cause. And, simply put, that is the self-conscious mind.

To rid one's life of discord, lack, difficulties and pain, which are all external conditions, the root cause must be defined and dealt with. The root cause is your thoughts that exist in the self-conscious mind. Millions of thoughts enter your mind, these thoughts are neither true nor false, they are just thoughts. However, you will be able to determine which are positive and which are negative; you will be able to sift out which make you smile and which bring you sadness. So the self-conscious mind needs to weed out all negative thoughts that does not serve the human and let it go. It will then look for all thoughts that bring about feelings of love, peace, happiness and fulfilment and embrace these positive thoughts for when it does this; it sends these thoughts to the sub-conscious mind. The sub-conscious mind, being a humble, faithful servant accepts these thoughts as the human's belief and brings it to pass.

Through this, it creates your reality and the life you live. The law of life is the law of belief. A belief is basically a thought in your self-conscious mind attached to an emotion that has been fed to the sub-conscious mind as true and then brought to life by the loyal sub-conscious mind, which makes no judgement and does not question your belief.

Your sub-conscious mind can inspire you, strengthen you and change your life completely, no matter what your circumstances may be. It is a state of pureness and peace. You just need to become aware of and change your thoughts in order to create your reality of fulfilment and blessed living. It is important to note that once the sub-conscious mind accepts a thought, it begins to execute it.

It is, however, the responsibility of the self-conscious mind to choose wisely as it has been given the gift of choice. The greatest power that you possess is the power to choose. So choose prosperity, choose success, happiness, enlightenment, perfect health and fulfilment.

Do not misunderstand your mind - it is not evil. No force of nature can be identified as evil. It just needs to be utilised in ways that serve you. If you are finding it difficult to control the thoughts in your self-conscious mind, think about the life that you desire. Imagine the success, the prosperity and the health that you want to experience for the rest of your life. Do not allow fear, worry and anxiety to take over as they interfere with the functionality of the sub-conscious mind. If you tell yourself "I will never make a success out of this business and I am always short of money in what I do" This is a negative self-conscious thought. And if you believe that this is true, the sub-conscious mind will obediently accept this and for a long time in your life, your business will not be successful and you will find that you are always short of money even whilst you are working. Can you see the consequences of your thoughts and beliefs?

Here are perfect examples of limiting self-conscious thoughts and beliefs:

- "I am always getting sick, I visit the doctor at least once a month"
- "It doesn't matter how many times I send out my CV, I still don't get interviews!"
- "My father will never approve of anything that I do, he has a problem with me"
- "I cannot afford to buy that, I do not earn enough"
- "My relationships never work, there is always drama and unhappiness, I don't think I was cut out to be loved or give love"

These are all limiting beliefs that do not serve you. Do they sound like they serve you? To me, each one seems like you are well on your way to creating a life of misery, anxiety, stress, ill health and loneliness.

If you make a conscious decision to change these limiting thoughts, however, these beliefs will fade away as you begin to embrace more positive ones. Through that, you will begin to harness a life of true beauty and success.

Change these limiting beliefs with the following affirmations:

- I am grateful for my perfect gift of health, which keeps me alive and allows me to work, live and be happy. I have been made perfectly and beautifully and I accept that my body is perfect just as it is. I have excellent health. I will be fine. I believe that I am a healthy human being. I am grateful that I can access excellent medical care when I need it, and I can keep my health because it is a gift.

- I am grateful for the opportunity to submit my CV for work opportunities. I firmly believe that I will receive a job that is fulfilling and successful. I trust the process of life. I accept that the good that is meant for me will be for me as I have faith. I am deserving of work and income.

- I understand that my father has limiting beliefs and I forgive him for it. I accept that I am perfect the way I am. I believe that in due time, he will understand me. My relationship with my father *will* be restored.

- I am deserving of a life of abundance, success and fulfilment. I believe that I will afford any item that which my heart desires for. The universe will open its doors to me and I will attract abundance, as I believe that I am worthy of receiving and I trust the process of God and life.

- I believe that I am perfect for the heart that is meant to love me. I accept and forgive myself for my flaws as I am human and it is okay. I deserve unconditional love and I will love unconditionally. The person I am meant to be with will soon enter my life and I believe that I will experience unlimited happiness and joy.

So you see what you have just done? You have consciously changed your negative limiting beliefs to positive affirmations, which will in turn bring to you a reality of all things beautiful. It is because you have realised that whatever you think about and believe to be true, you bring about and it becomes the life you live.

Unlocking the Treasures that lie Within

The most fundamental activity in the life of a human is building the mental spheres of your mind. You need to embrace the reality that there is Infinite Intelligence and Power that exists within your sub-conscious mind. You need to allow this to surface.

Many people believe that dreaming is something unreal. For example if I say: “I want that red Ferrari” and my friend adds: “dream on”…what is this friend saying? He is expressing that my dream is unreal, and his response immediately attaches a negative connotation to my dream, deeming it impossible for him to attain, and perhaps even for me.

But, if we take time to dissect this idea, you will soon realise that a dream is as real as an organ in your body. It is as real as you feeling with your fingers. A dream is a visualisation. When you visualise something, for example “I visualise myself travelling the world from the age of 30. I picture myself in different countries, inspiring people, exploring destinations and sightseeing”.

To many, this may seem like a dream. Something unreal. But to me, it is my visualisation. It is very real. It is what I want. It is what I think about. It is what I believe. These thoughts are impressions in my mind; these impressions will become a reality in my objective world due to the fact that it exists. This is when I say never underestimate the power of your thoughts.

If you wish to unlock the treasures that lie within you, begin by becoming an engineer of your thoughts. Grasp the concept of power of these thoughts. Make a conscious decision to believe that anything that you want in life can and will be yours if it is backed by faith and firm belief. When you are in a difficult situation, the first instinctive action of a human is to pray. If someone is on the verge of losing his job, he will turn to his

Creator, the Infinite Intelligence of the Universe and pray. He will pray to God asking, in fact begging God to please save him from losing his job. And his prayer will go along the following lines:

"Dear God, I am going through great difficulty, I am in a situation in my life that does not serve me and I need your help. I am about to lose my job. Please God, please save me from this predicament. I need my job. I need this income for my survival. I humbly ask you to help me dear God, please send me a miracle. I need you now more than ever in my life. I know you will help me God. I trust you God. You have never let me down before and I believe that you will help me in this situation in my life. Thank you God. Thank you so much".

Indeed a prayer from the heart directly to God. If you go through this prayer slowly, you will find that the person praying is firstly relating his problem to God, he then goes on to asking for help and further moves on to affirming his trust and his belief in God to put this situation right.

And indeed, God will help him. His job is saved. Now, I need you to understand something here. God exists within us. He is with us with each waking day of our life. He is closer to us than our jugular vein. He loves us seventy times more than our own mother. He is the Infinite Intelligence and Power that lives within us. He does not will any bad into our lives. He only brings purity, peace and everything blessed in abundance. If we are able to realise this and rise above a higher level of consciousness, we will come to understand that what we believe in, will become true.

This person believed that God will help him but he doesn't realise just how much he has helped himself by believing that his job will be protected. You cannot ask for help if you do not really want it. Likewise, you cannot allow your self -conscious mind to be possessed by ill thoughts of financial lack, fear of the future and worry from the past. Once you believe it, the sub-conscious accepts it and brings it to life.

Many people blame God for everything that goes wrong in their lives. And the funny part is many people blame other people for their difficulties. They are always seeking external factors to justify the life they created for themselves. Isn't it easier to blame someone else rather than take responsibility?

When you have the ability to look within yourself, unlock the doors to each room within the two spheres of your one mind, you will find the answer to every question you have or will ever ask yourself in your life. Nobody else will ever give you the right answer.

Within us, our true, non-judgemental self sits. This true self loves you, accepts you, forgives you and embraces you for who you are because you are pure, beautiful and unique. This true self cannot see any fault in you. It sees perfection, flawlessness, perfect health, love and happiness. This true self will continue to give you signals and signs in your life to find it. It will never go away until you are able to wake up from your deepened sleep and become conscious of its existence. This true self is very much alive within you and waits patiently for the day you are able to see it for what it is. And when that day comes, your life will change forever. You will come to many realisations. You will reach new states of thought. You will become an enlightened soul and you will no longer want or need immediate gratification in your life for anything whatsoever because you will find a state of mind that is true, sincere and filled with love. And it is from this point, that you will create the success you desire. You will not sabotage yourself again. You will realise the damage you have done thus far by being controlled by the thoughts of your self-conscious mind. You will unlock the treasures that lie within.

The sub-conscious mind is your protector. Just as God protects you and you are aware of this, as I said earlier, in my opinion, God exists within your sub-conscious mind and therefore your mind will protect you. It is the builder of your body.

Your Right to Riches

I have yet to meet anyone who has ever said: "I don't need any more money, I have enough". It's a fact that no matter how much money you have, it will never be enough, because we spend money. Also, our belief about money determines how much money we will have in our lives - what we believe will manifest as reality. The sub-conscious mind is powerful. The beliefs about money that are embedded into the sub-conscious mind are the exact degree to which you will receive money.

You do not have to work hard for money - you need to be smart about what you believe about money. Many people believe that money is the root of all evil. Others believe that money brings pride and arrogance into lives and, some even believe that money was not meant for them and, through that, they are stuck in their negative beliefs about money. They feel undeserving of money and impress to their sub-conscious mind that money is not good for them. The result speaks for itself. Depending on how much money you have right now in your life, it will give you a clear indication as to what your thoughts, beliefs, actions and behaviour is, where money is concerned.

In order to receive wealth in your life, you need to ensure that your sub-conscious belief about wealth has been built correctly, because your belief becomes your reality.

You must tap into the power of your sub-conscious mind and believe that you will experience wealth and success. You must believe that you are worthy of receiving wealth and success. You need to remove all negative belief about wealth and success from your sub-conscious mind.

You may have come across a person in your life that has a mediocre background, where he survived a rough childhood, perhaps even poverty. Yet today, that person is a millionaire who owns several businesses and is living a life beyond your comprehension. He has made it to this place focused on his own belief.

He believed that he deserved wealth and success. He did not think about the poor background or rough childhood. He steered forward with thoughts of wealth and success. Those thoughts were in his self-conscious mind. He continued thinking those thoughts until he believed it enough to embed it into the sub-conscious mind and the sub-conscious mind being a faithful servant with Infinite Intelligence and Power, accepted these beliefs as true and brought it to pass.

Another very important contribution towards receiving the wealth that you desire is gratitude. As I mentioned earlier in Chapter One, nothing you do in your life is without gratitude. Although the millionaire wanted wealth and success, at the same time, he had expressed gratitude for all that he was already blessed with in his life. Once you are grateful for that which you already have, you may continue to strive towards that which you still want in your life. Your thoughts, beliefs, actions and behaviour all contribute towards creating the wealth and success that you desire.

It is important to understand that there is an abundance of wealth in the Universe. God does not say "I will make this man rich and I will make that man poor"; "I will give you everything your heart desires and I will give him less"; " You will have poverty and starvation and he will have an abundance of wealth and prosperity" God loves all mankind equally. He only wills good things into our lives. He only wants what is best for us. He does not make decisions to give us a difficult life filled with suffering. It is each one of us that brings any situation unto ourselves.

God has blessed us with the power of choice. He has blessed us with the power of our sub-conscious mind, a place where He exists within us. We have, within us, the power to create a life that is fulfilling and successful. The life that we live is determined by our mind-sets. Prayer is a very important part of every person's life. It is when we open our hearts and our minds to our Creator speaking to Him directly and here we thank and we ask. Prayer can hold no purpose and be meaningless if it is not supported by belief. Belief is the law of life.

With belief comes emotion. The sub-conscious mind is the seat of all emotions. If I believe I am a successful person or I am a wealthy person, this belief is accompanied by a feeling. So not only do I believe that I am successful, I feel successful in all that I do. I feel like I have accomplished something in my life. I awake with the feeling of success together with the feeling of gratitude and in doing so, I am paving a way of even greater success in my life but my greatest efforts are not concerned with its results.

My beliefs and thoughts are true and sincere. And through them, my reality occurs. Wealth will come into my life from places that I have never, in my wildest dreams expected it to come from. Success will happen to me without too much of an effort from my side except for an infinite sense of belief.

Many people have said that they began to believe and convince themselves that they deserve wealth and success and months and even years passed and nothing happened. The reason for this was because there was contradiction and conflict between the belief and the feeling. They believed that they were worthy but they didn't feel worthy. When you have duality between a belief and a thought, the result is not clear. The interaction between the self-conscious and sub-conscious mind must be harmonious. Any single negative thought from the self-conscious mind brings about emotions of fear and anxiety. Fear and anxiety then produce limiting beliefs, obstacles and delays for you to receive what you deserve. You have placed these limitations in your life.

Your beliefs about money must always be pure. You must realise that money is a by-product of your true purpose. Once you understand what your true purpose is and work towards fulfilling that purpose, you will receive money because you are focused on your belief of fulfilment.

When you make a conscious decision to align your thoughts, beliefs and emotions harmoniously, remember to do it from a place of love and power and not from a place of fear or scarcity. You must become desensitised towards money.

I know someone who loves money. Although she loves money, she believes that money is hard to come by. She continuously says that she has to work very hard for her money and for that reason; it is not that easy to part with it. She knows exactly how much she receives each month, makes notes of every bill and keeps the remainder of her money in a savings account. She does not spend on anything that she does not need. She does not spoil herself even if she really wants something. And, she keeps her money safe. This is a perfect example of what her life will continue to be. Due to her limiting beliefs about money and how she needs to carefully count each penny, she will always earn the exact same salary for many more years in her life. She will never earn any more than that. She will continue in her thought and belief pattern. She will still be working in her old age and never truly experience the wonders of money or understand its true purpose in her life. She is emotionally attached to money believing that she has to work hard for it. She cannot spend it as she pleases.

Little does she realise that you cannot be emotionally attached to money – it is just paper and metals! Money is merely a by-product of your true purpose in life. It is paper that allows you to barter and receive goods in return. When you understand that you are not a receptacle, you are a conduit, you will begin to allow money to flow to and through you and not just to you.

When you are able to emotionally detach yourself from money, you will soon realise that you have decoupled yourself from the numbers. When you receive money in your life, accept it, be grateful for it and be in a state of mind that is happy to let it go as well. As you receive, let it flow out to others. As it flows away from you, it will continue to flow right back to you. This is supported by the belief within your sub-conscious mind. You believe there is enough for you and everyone else in the Universe. You believe that the more you give, the more you will receive.

Attracting more money into your life begins with a wealthy mind-set. A wealthy mind-set begins with a positive self-conscious thought. The thought must be of your true purpose, fulfilment, wealth and success. The thought must be of pure nature, embracing money yet not becoming emotionally attached to it understanding its role in your life. The thought must be of happiness, consistency and complete understanding that money flows through us and not to us.

The thought will then become a belief. Once it is a belief, you can attach emotion to it. These emotions of gratitude for what you have already been blessed with bring love, power, happiness and fulfilment. Your thoughts, beliefs and emotions are well presented in your behaviour. You will begin to behave in a grateful manner, you will embrace money as it enters your life, and you will wake up each morning feeling successful and wealthy.

Through this, your behaviour become actions and money will begin to flow through your life. As you receive this abundance of wealth, you will not be surprised. You will completely understand that you have followed and will continue to follow a process of thought unleashing the power of your sub-conscious mind to bring abundance into your life.

Self Help & Assessment Exercises

Chapter Two: A New Consciousness

1. Write down all of your current beliefs regarding the following areas of your life:

My Health, My career, my financial life, money, my relationships, my home life, love life

Now, write down your current, in this moment, thought about each of the above.

> For each of the above area, write down 1 positive action and 1 negative action that you have done where this area is concerned be it in the past or present moment. Remember to be honest with yourself.

Now for each area, begin to compare your thoughts, beliefs and actions and see where they are the same and where they are different. Once you identify the contrasts between your thoughts and beliefs, you must begin to re-align them so that they are the same for example:

Money – thought – I think that I should have more money in my life

Money – belief – I believe that I don't deserve more money in my life

Money – action - I sit at home all day waiting for someone to call me in for an interview

So as long as you're thought and belief does not resonate with each other, your action will always prove that which you believe to be true. You will impress confusion to your conscious mind, which makes it very difficult for the sub-conscious mind to produce the results of bringing money into your life.

So this exercise is great to help you first identify areas in your life and then attach your thoughts and beliefs to it and then make a conscious decision to act upon it and behave in a manner which provides clarity about what it is you want in your life.

Chapter Three

Dissolving the Illusory Fear

"Whatever frightens you, go for it! Go into your fear. Silently enter into it, so you can find its depth. And sometimes it happens that it is not very deep'

- Osho

Successful Leader Insight – Mr Salim Cassim, CEO, Apex Asphalt Construction

Tell us a little about your beginnings?

I grew up in the 5th most polluted area in the World, South of Durban, surrounded by 2 Oil Refineries, a Paper Mill, numerous Chemical Companies and not forgetting noise pollution, the Old Airport was our neighbour and you guessed it - the suburb of Merebank. We are a family of 6. From very humble beginnings, my parents worked extremely hard to educate all of us; Alhamdulillah we now have 2 doctors, 2 chemists, an ICU nurse and myself (civil engineering contractor)

What is your definition of success?

There is an old Latin school saying: Nil Shine Labour; translated into Nothing is achieved without hard work. Success for me is my family; I have 4 beautiful sons, a beautiful supporting wife and great staff. With a great combination of the above nothing is impossible. Success is inevitable.

What makes you a leader?

Leading from the front, making those hard decisions and the pressure of having 9 Franchisees who look to me for guidance…it's imperative to remain brutally honest yet gentle and caring towards other people's feelings. You cannot be autocratic as a leader. I'm a good listener,

take advice from everyone and then make the decisions, sometimes good or bad - nobody is perfect!

What advice do you have to offer young aspiring entrepreneurs?

Advice to other young and old entrepreneurs: Have BIG DREAMS!!! Don't let anyone tell you that you cannot do it, have a GOAL and work towards it, never give up, always strive to do your best in whatever you do in LIFE.

What kind of mind-set do you have? Tell us a little more about your thoughts and how they affect your life?

I am very curious by nature, looking at how things work, finding solutions to everyday problems, I invented an automatic feet dryer in conjunction with 3 dermatologists to cure athletes foot problems that we experience in the Gyms, ablution areas etc. a person is never old to learn, from the cradle to the grave, if you see a problem in life, try to fix it, I'm working on a book on the Reserve Bank, why does Inflation have to Exist? Very interesting research that I conducted over 19 years ago, want to share with the World what I have learned. The biggest challenge that I see, ourselves here in South AFRICA, huge inequality between haves and the have not's, didn't want to call it rich or poor, how we bridge the gap, As a parent I'm very concerned about what legacy we leave for our children, do we care enough about our fellow South Africans to Share our resources not only charity but beyond that, our skills as entrepreneurs, our ethics our culture and our roots.

Exploring Fear

I want to begin this chapter by asking you what your understanding of fear is? Is fear something real? And if it is real, can you touch it? Can you see it? Can you bring it in front of me this moment?

Take a look at these three scenarios:

- You receive news that the company that you work for is retrenching staff. Immediately, fear grips you, questions rise in your mind and you feel overwhelmed with anxiety. You could lose your job and this petrifies you.
- You've undertaken a work project but have not been able to complete it. The deadline day has arrived, you're about to present on your work and it is not up to your standard. You're scared,

you're nervous and you're convinced your presentation is going to be a failure.

- You recently opened up your new business and your first client agrees to meet with you. Fear invites itself over as you worry over saying the right thing, failing to get the work or you are unable to complete it?

Can you see the pattern? These are all unique situations but the common denominator is the feeling of fear. So again, I will ask. What is your definition and understanding of fear? Is fear something real?

Fear is as real as your shadow. Your shadow does indeed exist, because you can see it – but it is insubstantial. Every one of us has fear within us. People are afraid of the feeling of fear itself. Fear shakes our foundation because we are aware that it exists. The foundation shaking is very real, however fear is as real as a shadow. Although I have described 3 different scenarios above, there is only one feeling of fear.

When fear surfaces, it cannot be physically held in your hands or seen with your eyes but it is felt in your mind and expressed by your body with action and behaviour. Your palms become sweaty, your hands tremble and your body temperature changes completely. When we have fear, it is clear that we are ignorant of who we really are. We are afraid of our own selves. No matter what situation you experience that brings about fear, the main thought and belief within you stems from your fear of death.

I have had several experiences in my own life that made me fearful. The very same symptoms, thoughts, beliefs, actions and behaviour occurred. The fear that I had did not allow me to progress or grow on any level. It made me hesitate. It made me feel insecure. It made me feel as if I was in danger and I needed to protect myself. I did not quite know what I needed protection from but that was the predominant thought in my mind.

When I was younger, the biggest fear I ever experienced and this happened many times during the course of the year, for many years, was fear for my school examinations. Instead of concentrating on studying, my mind was more focused on thoughts about when I will be writing the exams. As a result, I felt tense and fearful. I was afraid of the questions, the results I would receive and I became so captivated by this fear that I was unable to sleep.

Then the day arrived, and it was time to write the examination. Fear, at its peak, and a rollercoaster of emotions accompanied me as I sat down to write the examination was at its peak. However, what I didn't understand at that time was, during the exam, whilst writing the actual paper, there was no fear. I was calm. I was fine. All fear was lost.

So, in essence, it is clear that fear is an emotion that we experience about a particular situation prior to it actually happening for when it does happen, the fear itself disappears and we find ourselves in the situation living it and getting through it fearlessly.

If there is something that you wish to do in your life or something that you wish to accomplish, you will naturally experience fear, because the consequences scare you. Fear is very much linked to the ego because the ego identity within you needs fear in order to strengthen itself. If you are not living in the present moment and if you are not accepting of what is, then you will experience fear and when you experience fear then you strengthen the ego within you. You relinquish all accountability to the fear that exists within you and you will realise as your life passes you by that it is fear itself that stopped you from doing many things in your life, from reaching goals and dreams, from fulfilling your vision and true purpose and from even loving and caring for people without conditions.

Many people are afraid of being alone. They always want to be in the company of others, and prefer to be out and about socialising. It seems like a glamorous way to live, to the observer and may even ignite a sense of inferiority within the casual onlooker.

Looking on, we may think: "look at her, she is so good with people and networking, always in the limelight, always in the company of people". Through thinking like this, you deem yourself less worthy of the "socialite".

The surprise for you, however, lies in realising that the very same person you admire, is actually quite scared. And what is it that they are so afraid of? You may be surprised to know that they are afraid of their own selves. They are afraid of being in their own company and spending time alone, in isolation.

Why would anyone be afraid to spend time on his or her own? Because there is silence, and only your thoughts to keep you company. Those thoughts force you to look within yourself, and, when this happens, you may discover that you're unhappy with what lies within.

When you look within, you may bring out things from within which you do not wish to confront or deal with and that can seem scary. Those who look within, awaken. And I must tell you that no matter how long a time you take to run from yourself and no matter how much fear you have to be alone and be in isolation, life is such that God will ensure that at some time in your life, no matter how old or young you are, at some point, you will have to look within. You will have to let go of the fear to look within and it is only then that you will realise who you truly are at the deepest level. And it is only then will you have the ability to understand your fear and manage it.

Fear is a by-product of your identity. When one is in a relationship, the most dominant emotion in that relationship may be fear - a fear of losing the person you love. When one opens up a new business, the most dominant emotion is fear - fear of the business being unsuccessful. As positive as you may be, as hopeful as you are, fear is fear is always there.

You may also be in denial when it comes to fear. I have heard many people say to me "I fear nothing and nobody but God" and this is profound. It is not, however, what you feel and believe to be true. Remember that emotions are attached to beliefs that come from a thought. So although you may think you are not fearful, if your thoughts and your beliefs are not aligned, you are in denial.

Fear is not something that can be destroyed. If you try to destroy fear, you will give it more power to exist within you and surface at another stage even stronger than before.

A few years ago, I moved into a beautiful expensive upmarket home in another city. I loved my home and I appreciated it but I lived in fear of losing it. I would think: "I am so young yet live in a luxurious home. What will happen if I cannot afford to pay for this one day? Where will I live? What will I do?" I had fear. I was grateful but today, I realise that my gratitude was thoughts and not beliefs. I thought I was grateful but I did not believe I was grateful.

Fear gripped me. It was many months later, when I made the decision to move back to my hometown that I realised that I was perfectly fine without living in that home. I adjusted to the next situation in my life. Human beings have been created with a gift to adjust to any circumstance, any situation and absolutely any difficulty that life presents to us. God has gifted us in this way with the ability to endure and adjust. As usual, I adjusted and found a home that may have not been as big and beautiful as that one, but it definitely made me feel more comfortable and dissolved the fear.

Think about it. How many times have you heard someone say "I don't know how I will live without my spouse/child/mother" or "I don't know what would happen to my life if I lost my job" and even the likes of "I cannot begin to imagine what my life would be like if I had to fall ill"

All of these comments are said from a place of fear. Not knowing what will happen to you will naturally bring fear into your mind and therefore your words and actions. But, consider this:

Have you seen people who lost their spouse/child/mother? Have you seen people who lost their jobs and even lost their health? What happened to them?

They were filled with fear but when the situation presented itself in their lives, they adjusted to it. The fear no longer exists because it is happening now. Anything that is happening in the present moment does not have fear in it. Fear is associated with the ego and the ego is diminished in the present moment. So no matter what happens in your life in the present moment, you will not experience or feel fear. You will only ever feel or experience fear when you are thinking about the future of something that is still to happen.

And if you have to dissect what I just said, I would ask myself: "How foolish am I? Firstly, the future does not exist for me yet. So I am fearful of something that does not exist. Secondly this future, this event that *may* happen in my life, which I am scared of, is going to become my present moment and in any present moment, fear does not exist. So what am I actually really afraid of?"

If you lose someone you love, God provides you with patience, acceptance and understanding in the present moment when you received news of the death. You still manage to pull yourself together and make funeral arrangements or contact close family and friends. You pray for the one whom you have lost. You say things like "He/she is in a better place, May he/she rest in peace. I trust that God is taking good care of him/her" You say these things. You believe these things. You trust God.

If you lose your job, you find another one. If you are too lazy to find another one, you will adjust your lifestyle so that it is affordable for you but the point is you adjust and take action. Whether it is consciously or unconsciously, whether in truth or denial, you do it. So what exactly are you so afraid of? What you are afraid of is the expectation that something may happen, and that expectation is based on past experiences of your own or others. Fear is therefore based on something that *has* already happened, and *that* situation does not exist anymore, and, it is based on something that *may* happen, and that situation does not exist yet. Either way, your fear is based on things that do not exist. In our society, we classify people like this as crazy.

The Mystery of the Unknown

Everyone yearns for security in life. What kind of security? Financial, so that you can pay the bills and feed yourself. Yet, even when we have a job or a successful business, we yearn for even more security, and ensure that you and your family are safe in the future. How would you feel if I tell you right now that having any idea of security is foolish on your part? I probably am getting you all worked up right now, aren't I?

The notion of security is an illusion. It does not exist. The very present moment does.

Animals do not seek out future security, as they seek or create shelter for their lives as it is at that moment. Flowers do not grow and blossom and look to continue to do so. They merely seek out the sunshine and then die. Animals and flowers serve their purpose on the Earth without looking for a future security. They find their security in their existence.

Humans have a tendency to desire security. When we realise that we will return to earth, taking nothing at all with us, in our natural states of being, then only will we have the ability to let go of the idea of security. And when you are looking for security, you have fear within you. No matter how much you may plan your life to be secure, the more you plan, the sooner God makes you realise the beauty of life and your existence. You may have heard of many stories where people have never smoked yet died of a heart attack, always took extra special care of their family yet lost a child in an accident or maintained a healthy diet but died of a fatal illness. Where is the security? Where is all the fear that you had of lack and loss? How did it serve you? In fact, to me, it seems that the fear actually attracted all of these unkind experiences into your life.

At this point, I want to ask you something. Although you may not be able to destroy or master the fear within you, at least try to understand that it does not serve you. Do not try to overcome it. Just understand it. When you are able to understand what fear is, you will be able to understand what you are not.

Fear cannot be eliminated from your life. It is as real as a shadow, because it exists but is insubstantial. It is when you discover your true self that you will be able to understand it. There are two things in your life that only you will ever know about and experience, and those are life and death.

Your life is only yours to experience, just as your death will be an experience only you go through. There are no right or wrong answers when it comes to your life and death as your unique experience cannot be understood are gone through by anyone else but you. Yes, there are opinions, beliefs, modes of thought about life and death but the only person who can experience your life is you.

We all want to survive, even thrive, in this world. By thriving, we wish to acquire wealth and success. As mentioned in a previous chapter where wealth and success are seeds of thought and belief planted into the sub-conscious mind. But, what happens when the voice within you tells you to do nothing?

Just to be. What's the worst that could happen, if you did nothing, if you did not react to a situation? When I say nothing, I do not mean sit and do nothing and expect business and wealth to flow into your life. Do not be mistaken - you must put effort in to accomplish things. I am talking about when the mind is so preoccupied with thoughts, desires and fear of the future and then suddenly silence. Nothing. What happens to us? We are unable to deal with it and we seek out noise to fill our minds with.

Don't do it. Ignore the noise created by anxious thought and embrace the nothingness. Welcome the silence and know that in its very existence is something even more powerful for you to grasp. You cannot grasp this unless you embrace the silence and the nothingness and become one with yourself. Slowly, fear disappears from within you. When you have the ability to look within yourself and open yourself up to the fear, then fear is lost. Remember that fear is born out of fear and fear creates more fear. When you are in a state of nothingness in your mind, you have embraced the present moment and you have let go of the idea of fear, effectively and entirely removing it from your mind.

Life is beautiful because it is insecure. It is a fleeting experience and a mysterious journey we have no true control over, because death exists within it. You cannot live without dying. Life can become a prison for many people who live in fear of what is yet to come, instead of living in the present moment. The only security and the only protection you will ever find or have in your life is God.

To everyone who fears the unknown, I ask: What exactly do you fear? Are you afraid of something, yet do not know exactly what it is?

That seems foolish. What would happen if you replaced that fear with love? If you began to love the unknown, your fear of it will disappear.

<u>The Inner World vs. the Outer World</u>

"Move within but don't move the way fear makes you move" - Rumi

Jalaluddin Rumi was a great poet who lived some 800 years ago. His wisdom and teachings have enlightened many hearts and minds, including my own. When he says "move within and but don't move the way fear makes you move", he is speaking of love. By moving the way that love inspires you to, you will move towards the light, a place of calm and peace. This is love - this is not fear.

Fear is an external experience because it manifests itself in your life's reality. If you are living a life where you do not have sufficient income, you are scared of not affording that which you might need. What do you do when trapped by fear? It's an internal feeling but it is entirely based on an external experience.

In order to overcome the fear that is brought into one's life based on external conditions, you have to do the inner work.

A child is born into this world without fear, and with complete trust. An infant is born believing that they will be cared for, as their natural instincts provide their caregivers with the indication of their needs. A child is born because it is not scared of what happens in life – it has no experience of fear, because its existence is a manifestation of love, hope and God's plan.

But, as that child grows into an adult, fear is instilled into its mind. The joy and bliss that were so evident at birth, is no longer a natural state of mind. It is something that that child now an adult has to search for and seek in things like meditation and other forms of spiritual activity.

Why not be in bliss and joy at all times? Why not trust God and trust the process of life at all times. If you do, what fear will you have? You cannot say you trust God and you trust life but you are fearful of what will happen? That is a contradiction. That is self-sabotage.

In order to create a life externally which will bring fulfilment, one has to look within oneself. When you make a decision to look within, you will no longer cling to anything outside of your existence. You will not cling to your home, your family, your relationships, your car and most certainly not money. You will become detached from those things, but they are still very much a part of your life.

To attain abundance though, you must be willing to go inward, without fear. With joy and happiness, go inward and find the nothingness that exists within you. Do not fear it. Embrace it. It will open up so many levels inside of you. It will bring about enlightenment. It will soften the heart. It will encourage love and give you a sense of peace and a feeling of fulfilment that you will never find in any external condition, person or material object.

It will give you the ability to trust life. You will begin to trust the process of life that has been ordained for you. You will replace all negative thinking with positive affirmations attracting only good into your life. You will trust and love God completely and understand that his plan is the best for your greater good. You will realise that the only security and protection you will ever need in your life is your trust in God and your gratitude for what he has blessed you with. The abundance will flow to you and through you. Your heart and your soul will open up magically and beautifully to everything and everyone around you. No circumstances or experiences in your life will be considered to be a problem and all fear will be dissolved. Fear will be replaced with love, trust and faith. You will no longer need to take control of the interaction between your self-conscious and sub-conscious mind, as it will happen naturally. Negative thoughts will leave your self-conscious mind. Your sub-conscious mind will only receive thoughts of gratitude and abundance and trust. It will manifest those things as your reality.

When you take time in your life to look within, you will find God within you. Do not be afraid to isolate yourself from others and the chatter of your mind. Find your inner nothingness and realise that your inner voice speaks silence.

When you are conscious of your inner world, your outer world will take care of itself. God does not will any bad into our lives and we create our own reality.

People are always in search of something, be it wealth, status, contentment and or security. All of these things are external conditions and anything you chase in the outer world will continue to evade you. It is only when you look within, let go of fear and give thanks for what you have, that life enables all your desires to be fulfilled in your outer world.

Most of all, when all of what you dream of becomes your reality, you will not be surprised. You will smile sweetly and know that you have created it. You will understand that it is a means to an end, and does not make you who you are. You will begin to trust that everything you require in life will always be there, and you will not be scared of loss. You will experience bliss and joy just as you did as a child. You will experience permanent meditation as all it is, is stillness of the mind. As long as you trust, you will not fear. As long as you love, you will not fear.

Time to let go

In the previous chapter, I spoke to you about the two spheres within your one mind. That is the self-conscious and sub-conscious. I would like to introduce another level of consciousness that exists within your mind.

Your conscious mind is the state of mind that has content in it. By this we mean that it is filled with needs, wants, desires and fear. You want wealth; you have greed, envy and desire for things and people in your life. You are attached to items and you cling to people seeking comfort and approval. That is the first conscious state of your mind.

The second conscious state of your mind is the one without content. This is your sub-conscious state of pureness. There is stillness, nothingness and light. There are all the things beautiful that are there to serve you. The sub -conscious controls all your vital processes and governs your body. In this second conscious state of mind, you find peace. Here, you will find yourself in a state of meditation and are able to express your true self.

The third state of mind that I would like to introduce to you is the super-conscious mind. Here, there is no need for consciousness. When you are conscious, you are aware of a thing, situation or thought. In this third state of mind, you exceed consciousness and simply exist.

There are no noisy thoughts, no fear and no anxiety. There is just silence and beauty. The super-conscious mind is where you exist, and where you realise you are a soul.

A soul can never die. Even when your body ceases to function and you die, your soul continues. Your soul comes from God and is returned to God. In your super-conscious mind, you understand that you are a soul, not a body, and you are not affected by life. Here, you are beyond thinking and the acts of living a human reality. In your super-conscious mind, you are your authentic, unaffected self.

The day you reach a stage where you can say "I am nothing" it means that you have come to a profound realisation. You are not your body, mind, thoughts or material existence. You are consciousness and you are nothing. When you die, your body will deteriorate, you will be placed back into the earth. You will become nothing but skeleton and bone. Then how real do you think you are? And when you die, you are taking nothing with you. Not a single thing. Then how important are those things now in your life?

I am going to ask you to try this significant life changing exercise. Take something, any item that you truly value and hold a deep sentimental feeling towards.

Once you identify what that special item is, I am going to ask you to give it away. Don't sell it, trade it or throw it away. Simply give it away to someone else.

Once you do this, you will have a life transforming experience. You will reach a new level of consciousness. Don't be surprised by your own emotional response to this experience – you may experience joy, bliss and perhaps even cry over it. Not only will you tap into a space inside of you that you have never felt, but also you will realise that without that item, you still exist. Your worth has not been diminished through the act of giving away such a seemingly precious item.

By detaching yourself from that item that you held so close to your heart, you will realise that nothing owns you. You are allowed to own items and objects but they will never own you. The reality is many people live lives where they are owned by their possessions. They are so consumed by it that they hold on so tightly afraid to let go.

But what will happen if it is gone? Give it away and you will find out. Nothing. Nothing will happen besides an awakening inside of you. You made a decision to open the door to look within you and you will be amazed by the treasure house that lies within that will change your entire life.

The biggest problem with people, with humans is the inability to let go. They love to possess. If you have a grandmother who is still living, take some time to visit her. You may find she has items in her home that she has kept with her for years, maybe even generations. She identifies herself through those possessions. Little does she realise that her sense of identity and who she is was never related to what she owns and never will be. Her true self, her true existence and her true beauty were and are always within her soul and when she passes on, she leaves all of those possessions.

When she dies, we weep and pray for her. We miss her. What do we miss? We miss her character, her compassion and her love for us. We do not miss her possessions or her house.

The world is changing though, and we are all moving away from this possession-centred state. As generations pass, we actually find people desiring less throughout existence and human evolution.

Ask yourself – what am I holding on to? My house, car, cell phone?

Today I am driving a Mercedes. Tomorrow if that Mercedes is taken away from me, how will I face the world? What would people say? I feel I will be worthless if I am not driving this Mercedes. That is fear speaking, and fear is created because of my attachment to the car. I've identified myself, my worth and value through this car. But is this car my soul? Does my spirit live within the automobile? Of course not! It is merely fear that makes me think it does.

Let go, detach and hold on to nothing but God. How do you do that?

- Remain in a state of gratitude.
- Choose your thoughts carefully.
- Make a conscious decision to become a positive person and appreciate all that you have been blessed with.
- Think thoughts of prosperity, wealth and abundance.
- Do not attach yourself to the world of external conditions and objects. It will surely come to you, it must come, but only when you have resolved the conflict and the torment in your inner world. Only when fear is dissolved. Only when fear is replaced with trust and with Love.

I have met a few hard-hearted businessmen in my life. Their sense of identity is only found through their possessions, their wealth, their status and their power.

They live a life of falsehood. As powerful as they may seem to the world, they are actually very scared people within. They may think they've found the key to happiness through their wealth but true joy does not lie in their wealth. It never will, because God did not create us to become attached to anything. If he did then we would be buried with our cars, houses and our vaults.

God created us to enjoy the wealth of the world, but not to become emotionally attached to it. One cannot find one's identity in a building or a flower, but it is found within.

Be who you are, authentically, as you give love, stay humble and live a life of generosity. This makes your wealth and your success all the more fulfilling as you can only truly value wealth and success when you are a giver. When you are in a state of bliss and joy at all times, when you find happiness in everything else but your wealth, status and success, you will realise that they are just means, not your end. In the end of your life, you will have only you and you will need your true self. You are your true self. You will always be your true self. Your true self will never leave you. Life will throw at you many experiences until you wake up and look within and find your true self.

Whatever you place the most attention on in your life, that part will receive more of your energy, whether it is good or bad. The more you feel fear and the more you resist fear, the more strength you give to your fear. The more attention you pay to your fear where you continuously say, "I will not have fear, I will overcome my fears" The truth is that you absolutely will not.

Your sub-conscious mind pays careful attention to your thoughts, words, beliefs and emotions. The more you mention the word fear, the more you will feel fear. So why not replace the focus of fear and move towards focusing on love? Love can conquer any situation in your life.

If you have two clients and you want more, but seem to have been successful in your efforts to garner them, you may ask "what am I doing wrong?"

Well as long as you have not let go of the fear that you may not attract more clients, you will only have two clients. And if you have not expressed gratitude and love towards those two clients, you may even lose them, no matter how powerful your marketing techniques or how much work you put into their projects. Remember your thoughts and your beliefs must always be equally aligned and being grateful is part of the process just as love is. Changing your focus from fear towards love is the most powerful strategy you will ever need to accomplish any goal in your life.

The only reason an extremely wealthy businessman will become a hard-hearted person is because his heart is closed to love. When your heart is closed to love, it opens to fear.

There are only two ways to live your life – with fear or with love. If you do not know how to love, then you will certainly fear. When you fear, your heart hardens. When your heart hardens, you close yourself off completely to your inner true self. You will only live and find your identity in your outer world. You will only wish to control, dominate and possess everything in your life, and you'll be scared of losing it all.

If you live a life with love, you will relinquish all power unto God. You will trust God and trust His plan. You will let go of the fear that lives in your heart. You will love everyone and everything around you; continue to be successful in your business and every aspect of your life. This is because everything in your life is borne from love, not fear.

By now, depending on your age and experiences, I am certain that you may have met someone in your life who seems to be nothing less than perfect. They are intelligent, smart, beautiful, wealthy and successful - they appear to be everything you admire. It seems as though they were created perfectly and just continued to be perfect in all that they do. You may even fall in love with this person and your entire world would revolve around this 'perfect' person.

And then, for some reason, they are gone from your life. They leave you, or move on. You are left confused, hurt and perhaps even broken. You find yourself unable to concentrate on your career, your health or any aspect of your life, because you're so focused on the notion that they are no longer a part of it.

Let us take a closer look into this 'perfect' person's life. Because he has successfully exposed himself as this beautiful, perfect, successful human being does not necessarily mean that he had it altogether. Deep within him, there lived fear and a sense of distrust in himself. He is scared to look within because he may find emptiness and that scares him. But, as we now know from previous chapters, emptiness is a rather beautiful place to be in!

The 'perfect' person appears on the surface as smart, intelligent, beautiful and successful however if he cares to look within his own soul, unlock every door within his own heart and see what's inside, he will see past the mask that he wears. He will find purity.

But if he is afraid, that is not your fault. It is not as if he cannot look within, he must want to look within himself. He must let go of the fear of what he may find and unwrap it gently. It is only when he has done this, will he learn how to trust himself and trust God completely. It is from this point where he will have the ability to trust another human being and be able to love sincerely.

Unfortunately, what I have described above is the lives of many people but they live sadly in denial. And, as we know, denial is borne out of fear. A life lived with fear as its centrepiece will be one of denial, of ignoring one's true self and one of hurt.

Self Help & Assessment Exercises

Chapter Three: Fear

- Make a list of things of everything that you have fear of in any area of your life

- Identify at least 2 situations / experiences in your life that have happened in the past, which have brought about fear or anxiety within you.

- Identify at least 3 things that you could have achieved in your life but did not pursue due to fear of it being unsuccessful and not working out for you

- Identify 3 things in your life that you currently wish to pursue

- Write down what you have done thus far and what effort you have made towards each of the above items that you wish to pursue

- Identify any and all of the fears that you think, feel and believe that are standing in your way of achieving all of the above goals

- Close your eyes and begin to imagine yourself in the situation where you are experiencing all of the fears that you have mentioned above.

- Embrace the feeling of fear. Let it ignite every feeling and thought and even behaviour associated with fear.

- Now it is time to let go, slowly breathe in and breathe out allowing every feeling and thought associated to that fear to be released from your self.

- Affirm to yourself that it is safe to believe that you are capable of pursuing each one of your goals.

- Affirm to yourself that you are deserving and worthy of accomplishment.

- Affirm to yourself that you will make effort to pursue your goal, without hesitation

- Affirm to yourself that God is all around and within you and He is protecting you from all your fears like a shield. Affirm that you have been created perfectly and you will make a success of anything that you set your heart out to do. Convince yourself that it is safe to pursue your venture or idea or project, with firm faith and belief that it is going to work out perfectly fine and it will be a success.

- Believe that fear is nothing but a thought in your mind which you need to let go of and replace that thought with a trust and faith in your Creator

Chapter Four

Manage the Ego Self

"The haughty, even with pride equal to a mustard seed in his heart, will not enter paradise'

Prophet Muhammad (Peace Be Upon Him

Don't blame me, blame my ego

You are delusional if you say that you don't have an ego, for having an ego self is part of being human. Your ego is not something to hide or run away from, because it exists within you. The ego self is also known as the false sense of self. To me, the ego is the unconsciousness that is within you.

We all enjoy the finer things of life, like fancy cars or branded clothing. These items make us feel good about ourselves, and many people derive their sense of self from these material objects. But, as lovely as it is to desire and own luxury items, the question remains – do these define you?

But that's still a mild expression of the ego, for desiring external gratification through objects and possessions is not the full extent or expression of the ego self.

The ego exists within the self-conscious mind and through this is able to strengthen itself. A lot of the suffering in the world, over centuries and decades have been at the hands of collective ego. The ego has divided communities, blood relations, friends and even children. It has created disruption, suffering and misery over time and unless and until, mankind becomes aware of the ego and becomes more conscious about its danger, this vicious cycle of madness, separation and intolerance will continue for future generations to come.

We all possess a very personal sense of identification. Our identity document confirms our birth and it's through that document that we are able to access services, be identified and even vote in our country's elections. Through this document, we are proven to exist in the world.

And this document becomes "my" identity document. So you possess it, it belongs to you and it shows the world that you exist. The same goes for a child. A child has toys that are theirs, they attach themselves to their favourite toy and to the child, and it is "my" toy. Through possession, again, comes identification.

As we grow older as adults, we possess things in the world, whether they are a couch, car, house or any seemingly infinite combination of items. Through our possessions, we become identified. For example, a person would say "Don't you know him? He owns that successful company"

So, in essence through a few words and labels here and there, we are given our sense of self. This is who we are. But is that really true? Do the labels that life and people give you define who you are?

If the labels were taken away from us, what would remain? Is it safe to say that we are nothing? The truth is we are nothing with or without the words and labels. It may be a little difficult to comprehend this right now but let's continue.

Each of us has a voice in our head that talks to us. And of course, you think that this voice in your head is in fact you. It tells you that you need to strive and achieve and succeed. It tells you to do more, be more and get more. It even tells you that you are not doing enough and you need to put in more effort in your endeavours. Sometimes, this very same voice tells you that you are worthless. It says things to you that make you feel depressed or disappointed in yourself. This voice is even capable of making you lose all sense of self-worth or value. As much as it gives you power, it can also diminish you. The voice in your head also convinces you that you need things in your life in order for you to be recognised as important or successful. And on the same token, it makes you feel as if you are not good enough so you are on a mission to always seek and find gratification and self-worth and value from external conditions in your life. The perfect example is women and beauty products are it slimming or firming. Women are always in search of better products that can enhance their beauty and external appearance. There seems to be an incessant need to look younger, remain beautiful and feel approved of by others. For that reason, they invest in expensive facial and skincare products, clothing, bags, shoes and make-up to enhance their physical appearance. The media industry love this and their businesses thrive on this. They know that most women are insecure about themselves. In fact, most women are never satisfied with their looks or their weight. There is always complaint. There is always desire to want something better so that I can be better and feel better about myself. Sadly, the reality is that after the investment, give it a few months, and they are no longer satisfied. There must be something else that I need, that I want that will make me even better than what I am. So, enough will never be enough because there is a desire to better the self. And as long as you are on a mission to improve yourself externally and you are fixated on external improvement, the inner torment will continue.

Remember that this is not you. This is your ego. The ego lives within you and it derives its own sense of identification through you. It strengthens itself within you and it grows and will continue to grow for as long as you give it all of the power it needs to do so. In order for the ego to grow, it needs you to be attached to things. And when you become emotionally attached to anything, it becomes very difficult to let go of it. You have the perfect nourishment that the ego needs. Attachment.

The world is so focused on proving their value and their worth through identification of form that it is an absolute challenge to look within. In the previous chapter, I mentioned fear of having to look within. When you look within, you may find that it is empty and in most instances, it is empty. But what is wrong with emptiness? The fact that emptiness exists proves that it is not such a bad thing after all. Once you identify the emptiness, from that point can you develop self-acceptance, self-love and fulfilment? And when I talk about self-love and self-acceptance, please understand this. Many people will insist that they love their self and they accept their selves. And this is wonderful. The love and acceptance that I am referring to though is you without what you have. So if your possessions were taken away from you for example your beautiful clothing, your make up, your big fancy cars, homes and anything external that you find your sense of self in, if these were completely stripped away from your life and never to be returned, will you still love yourself? Will you still accept yourself? Has your worth and your values diminished once this has all been taken away from you? Are you no longer the same person or are you? Will people still give you the same respect and honour?

Let's understand a different side of the ego. There are many, many people in the world that don't have luxury. No fancy lifestyle. No attachment to material objects. They are able to exist and live an average life with the necessities. However, these people have egos that are ten times greater than those of some millionaires. Does this surprise you? Oh but it is very true.

These are men and women who don't need anything of material substance to strengthen their ego. The voice in their head is far too strong and powerful and dominating. The ego is not something you can let go of and destroy. It is like fear. I mentioned that you cannot destroy fear but you can understand it. So if you try to let go of material wealth to destroy your ego, you may not achieve this, simply because the ego will find other ways to exist within you. In fact, if you consciously choose to destroy it, it will try everything to become even stronger within you. What you fight will strengthen. So maybe fighting and destroying isn't really the solution here. The solution is awareness and consciousness. Having the ability to identifying the ego that exists and when particular situation or experiences take place in your life, then you will know whether it is your true self or your ego self that has reacted to that situation. It is having the ability to distinguish between the two and think carefully in any situation that life presents to you.

It makes no sense to try and let go of attachments. It is not quite possible. All that you are doing is changing the content of the ego but it is still there. It is funny how the opinions of other people affect our lives and our sense of belonging and identification. When we are accepted, respected or approved of in a community then we feel safe because we meet the criteria. Not only do we make more effort to prove our worth and our value, but also we will want to impress others more and more. The more we impress the more we become. The better we are. Oh and many people are not completely conscious of their actions and behaviour. It is something that happens by default.

I own a company. I now own a fancy car. I have respect from other wealthy people. I cannot be seen wearing this dress by that person. What will they think of me? I must maintain a certain look and style and I must even speak in a certain way in the presence of this person. Can you not see what you are doing? Can you not identify the power that your ego has over your true self? It becomes a daily challenge to stay true to you and it can be a nightmare. That vicious challenge of seeking approval and respect leads you to not risk things, not be true to yourself and it will continue to do grow.

The ego has within its character, dissatisfaction and incompleteness. These are its characteristics; this is what it is made up of. So if you think that you will feed your ego only until a certain part of you is fulfilled and then you will be true to yourself thereafter, you are mistaken. You will never achieve complete fulfilment. You will never be completely satisfied. You will always feel a void, a hole within you that needs to continuously be filled with something. And the more you try and fill it with things, the emptier it becomes. If you think that you are not emotionally attached to a person or a material item, then try giving it up. Give it up, give it away or walk away from him/her or it.

If it stirs any emotion within you of sadness, pain, anger, resentment or disappointment that is emotional attachment. If there is emotional attachment, there is a sense of identification of you through that person or object. If you require anything outside of your existence to make you feel worthy or valuable, you are living in a state of delusion and madness.

Let me give you an example. If you are in a relationship with a very attractive person, that person becomes the centre of your universe. Your thoughts, beliefs, actions and behaviour will change accordingly to be in tune with that person's life. You will find yourself starting to like all the things that person likes. You will find yourself in admiration and awe staring at the person you love. It is almost as if you begin to idolise your love. In many instances, people have sacrificed their own self-worth and their own values and morals for the sake of the other person, in the name of love and belonging. You feel that you can only exist through the love you have for that person. Many have said, "I will die if he/she leaves me, I cannot live without him/her" really? You cannot live without him? How did you live without him before he came into your life? Remember I spoke about the ability God has given man to adjust into any situation that life presents. Well, the truth is you will survive. You will live. And you will be fine.

But as long as you are consumed by another individual, as long as you have given up who you really are to find some sort of identification of yourself and your value through another human being, again you will always have a void and a hole within you that needs to be filled. The ego will make you think that you need to be attached to the person you love. The voice in your head will continue to torment you that you are nothing without that person. You will lose your worth. You will diminish.

And sadly, you give the voice in your head the power. Firstly, by accepting the voice as if it is your true self. And then by making sure you do everything in your power to keep your possession, which is the person, you love. You will sacrifice anything. You will do anything. You will forget about your own worth if need be. You become weak yet you think you are strong.

You will meet successful leaders in your life. They possess wealth beyond comprehension. There is nothing they are short of. They do not need people. They do not need love. They do not need friends or even family. All they need is their wealth. So these men and women attach themselves and their sense of identification to their thriving businesses. They awake and go to bed talking and thinking about their business. To them, nothing else matters. The only thing that matters to them is how will I make more money today? That is their highest value above all else. The challenge, however, arises when they no longer know who they really are. They have lost their sense of self and true pure character in this madness. The ego has taken over them completely. In fact the ego is so strong that it is controls everything in that person's life. It has become a disease.

It has become a parasite. It is victorious. As much as these successful individuals think and believe that they have done a great deal in this world, it is nothing but a veil of delusion. The day of their realisation will come. You see the ego exists and I keep saying do not try to destroy it but understand it. The ego is destined to die and to dissolve. This is the fate of the ego. It will serve its purpose but it is guaranteed to dissolve within the same person through which it received its strength. And this is a very crucial point to think about. You may think it is okay to allow your ego to grow and strengthen within you during the course of your life. Well age and health is on your side so why not right? However, you have not pondered much about what will become of you, of this shell that you dwell within also known as the body and then the mind, when the ego dissolves within you? Will age and health still be on your side? Let us pray to God that it is because you will need it.

It is okay to have a want and a need. It is perfectly normal to strive towards wealth and success. It is even better to continuously think and believe that you will be a successful leader and entrepreneur. And of course you must. You must open businesses, provide employment, take care of families and be respected for your wonderful efforts. You must even live a life of luxury. If you can afford to buy a fancy car and a beautiful palatial home then buy it. If you enjoy wearing branded clothing, then wear it. If you attain great pleasure in food then indulge. However, do not look for your sense of identity through this life. Understand that these are things to be used as a means; it is not the end all. It is not who you truly are at the deepest level. No amount of wealth or success can or will ever determine your true value and worth. Those are virtues that exist within you. Those virtues are what make you who you are, whereby, if everything is taken away from you, you will still be valuable to others. You will still be respected and treated well by others. The behaviour and attitude of people will not change, no matter what you own. This is when you know that you have become aware of the ego that is within you and in doing so; you now know who you are not.

Do you choose drama over peace?

How often have you encountered someone close to you or sometimes not, who is always falling ill. Every time you meet or speak to this person, there is some illness that they are suffering from. Sometimes, the illness even changes and perhaps becomes multiple issues - this week it could be a knee problem, next week it may be a head problem.

All of us experience illness during our lifetime, but this is an overwhelming attachment to illness, such that illness becomes a part of this person's identity.

When the ego cannot find anything else in you to strengthen it, it will continue searching until it finds something. There will always be something that it can attach itself to and grow. So many people become victims of their illness. Perhaps, they lack love and attention in their lives and it seems that the only way to receive love and attention from friends and family based on their tried and tested methods is through illness. And this does not mean that the illness is not real. The illness that they suffer from is very real. However their predominant thoughts and ego-centred belief is that when I am ill, I receive more love and attention. My ego needs that attention and because of that, illness becomes a part of who I am. The more I complain, the more ill I become, the more attention I receive. The more pity I need. When I receive attention and love, it makes me feel better about myself. I feel more worthy and more valued by those around me. In essence, you are looking for your self worth and acceptance externally, from your illness, from your friends, from your family.

If you look within, you will realise that God has created you beautifully. His own essence and existence is within you. No matter who you are, you are perfect to God.

You must love and accept yourself on all levels to such a depth where you will no longer need anyone outside of your own soul to make you feel better about yourself and if they do, well that is not a bad thing because it is not something that you do not already know. And if they don't, then that is also okay because you already know the truth. You already love yourself. You already accept yourself. You do not require external gratification or satisfaction. What happens then, is automatically, your sub-conscious mind no longer receives thoughts and beliefs about illness, it receives complete love and appreciation of oneself and the illness will not be able to manifest. Each cell within your body will exist in perfection and beauty, and will function in harmony with your soul. Your sub-conscious will maintain your health because it exists with positive energy and is filled with gratitude. When the illness dissolves, so does the ego that is attached to that illness. Now the ego has nothing to attach itself to and you are no longer a victim.

In Chapter One, I said that gratitude brings riches and complaint brings poverty. Complaining is one of the most effective strategies that the ego uses in the human mind. When you complain, you are dissatisfied. There is something or someone that you want and you do not have it. If you had it, you would be happy. Again, this is a delusion of the truth. The ego is very much conditioned by your past and your upbringing. For every experience that you have ever had in your life, the ego is aware of it. It has grown and developed through all of your past experiences so long as you were not conscious and aware of its existence. In an argument, both people that are arguing want to be right. They want to prove their point especially in business or relationship related matters. Your mind convinces you that you cannot and will not be defeated by the other person. You will say and do whatever it takes to ensure that you stand your ground because you need to be right. Being right includes a feeling of satisfaction, a feeling of victory and a sense of identification of who you are in the eyes of others. Proving your point means that you have not been defeated and you are not wrong. The question is what is being defeated? What is being made right or wrong? Is it you? Is it your true self or is it the ego that lives within you? It cannot possibly be your true self for your true self is a place of peace, calmness, neutrality and contentment. Why would your true self ever feel defeated or less worthy in any external situation? The true self is not attached to anything. The true self needs no convincing so it is not even you that wants to argue or prove your point - it is the unconsciousness in you. You are unconscious because if you were conscious you would say "Hey, there is nothing to prove, there is nothing to defeat, it does not matter what the other person thinks, let it be. I understand that the other person is unconscious and it is not really him or her that is arguing with me, it is his or her ego and I am aware of this so let me behave from a place of non-judgement, I choose to not empower my ego"

This cannot possibly; in anyway whatsoever make you any smaller. And if you think it does, if your mind wants you to believe that it does then ask yourself "Exactly how will it make me smaller? In what form and in what exact way?" There will be no answer, because you cannot become any smaller. You still are.

You still exist. Nothing has changed. The only thing that has changed is the thoughts in your mind. The only thing that has changed is that you have become aware of who you are not.

We are all living with fear from our past experiences. If I had to ask you to come forth and show me your past, what exactly can you show me? You can tell me stories using your imagination and I can choose whether or not I wish to believe you but how could you ever possibly bring your past forth and show it to me. That's just it. You cannot. Yet for years we have heard people saying repeatedly, you are carrying your past into your future. You have not yet let go of the past. You have huge baggage in your life. Really? Where is this baggage? Can I please see it? Do you mind showing it to me? This past. This baggage. This unresolved conflict. These are nothing but thoughts in your mind, that keep playing like an old movie on repeat. So basically, what you are carrying forward in your life is thoughts. Thoughts of what has already happened in your past that still have an effect on your beliefs and your emotions. As long as you allow and give complete permission to those thoughts, they will continue to strike emotions and beliefs in you. Your ego loves the idea that you are still thinking thoughts of the past. The ego enjoys every minute of when your mind takes you back in time and swallows you with thoughts which have emotions and beliefs attached to it. Especially when the thoughts, emotions and beliefs from the past are negative and damaging to your present.

I have yet to come across any individual who does not fight or argue with someone that they love or are close to. The famous saying goes "familiarity breeds contempt" so the closer you get to someone, the more likely you are to fight or argue with him or her. For some people, it becomes much more severe, it is not just a fight or an argument. It is verbal abuse, insults, continuous complaint and sometimes even physical abuse. Based on your own past experiences which you continue to dwell on, you will behave in unacceptable behaviour with people that you love and care for. Here, the ego needs to feed off another person and their negativity. So the best person that it finds is the one the human loves and cares for. In every relationship, be it a business or marital or even a parent and child, where there is intense love, it becomes almost like an obsession followed by pain.

Both parties will share a normal understanding and soon, there is some sort of pain inflicted on each other. The ego that exists within both people need to feed and there is nothing better than to feed off the negative energy which emanates from the other person. So, based on their pain from the past, they will seek trivial issues in the person they love and care of. Sometimes, there will be pain and suffering inflicted for the smallest and silliest reasons. Any opportunity to find a fault in the other person, start the argument and wait for the pain and suffering to be returned. Once it is returned, the egos energise. They feed. When they are satisfied, they go back into their dormant states. What happens in the relationship? Things go back to normal. The true self surfaces. Forgiveness. Love. Sympathy. All of your good virtues and qualities will surface until the ego awakens and becomes active again for more pain and torment.

The next time you find yourself stirring from within. Emotions of unhappiness, anger, dissatisfaction, and the eagerness to blame and to inflict pain because you feel that someone has hurt or upset you and you need to defend yourself or prove your point. Stop. Look within. Ask yourself "Am I doing this and am I feeling this or is it my ego that wants this right now?" Then move on to think about what will happen once it is all over. The thing we call consequence.

It will also become easier for you as you become more and more aware of what and who you are not that you will have the ability to identify the unconsciousness in other people. When they become angered, complain, blame or resent, you will stop and say "Hey hold on, that cannot be that person's true self, it must definitely be the ego. I forgive you because you are unaware and I will not retaliate. I prefer to remain silent". After some time, maybe even after a few occasions of what I just described, you will in a silent and subtle way, make the other person become a conscious human being without having to say anything to them. Which person will want to continue being angry and proud before someone who offers no reaction whatsoever? Just blank stares. Will you ever shout at a person that you know is completely deaf no matter how angry you are?

It is natural to become upset. It is natural to complain. Please, I understand that you are a human. I am too. I do the same thing as you. If we didn't, we would be up in the heavens with God, as his angels. They are perfect and beautiful. But then, so are we. I mean our true selves. However, we are also human and it is not as if we asked for ego to be part of us. We didn't place it on a request form. It exists. It is there. Now what? Nothing. Just be aware that it exists. Lose the labels of yourself - "I" own that building and that is "my" car. You exist therefore you are – you don't need to own anything to be. You just are. The car may be there but it is external. Even your body is external as it is a shell that you live within. When you die, it will diminish into the earth.

So how solid are you? How existent are you? Your existence is your soul. This soul is pure, divine and has been created with perfection by God. It needs no external force, item or circumstance to know its worth. Even after you die, it will exist. So why would you short-change yourself by seeking satisfaction in people and objects when your existence cannot even be compared to any possession whatsoever?

Your virtues and your qualities will remain and your ego will dissolve. You will never need human drama in your life and if human drama presents itself, you will be able to acknowledge it for what it is, overlook it and carry on. It will not define you or change you.

The Addiction of the Ego

In business, you will often meet like-minded people and the conversation surrounds business and networking and opportunities. Did you notice how if a really wealthy person's name is mentioned, the other person automatically "knows them personally" and will say things like "Yeah we are good friends, we had dinner together last week" or something along the lines of "Sure, I know him. In fact, we meet every other day, we know each other through family" It somehow seems that someone or the other is connected or related or friends with someone "very high up there". My point is - if you are friends with someone famous or rich, to what benefit is that bit of information in your business conversation? How relevant is it to the topic of discussion? Will it make a difference? Maybe you will receive the contract that was pending. Maybe you are now seen differently because you rub shoulders with someone rich and famous. Your association suddenly holds some relevance. You are no longer just an ordinary businessperson.

In several cases, the ego lies. Even if it does not know that specific man of wealth or fame, it will, at that moment, convince the human that it does and that's why the human lies. You lie and lose all fear of getting caught, because lying appears to be a better option at that time. Through that, you start believing the lies that you speak. So besides the fact that ego is now empowered, you have told a lie to gain credibility and recognition and in doing so, you believe the lie so now you are convinced that you are great friends with that person and guess what? The next time you might even speak the same lie again. Until the day finally arises, where reality hits you. Through some event or occurrence, the truth is revealed. Sometimes, it is only revealed to you, sometimes it is revealed in the presence of others. Feelings of embarrassment, humiliation, dislike of oneself will rise to the surface. Can you see that the ego will do whatever it takes to destroy your true sense of self? It will create discord and misery in your own life. However, it was only you who created this reality.

And the first thing we do when we create our own problems is to look outside ourselves, because it is easier than looking within. If we look within, we might even start to hate what we find inside of us. We may be afraid to unlock each door and look inside and unwrap our true selves. So we look outside and seek out someone or something to blame.

And trust me, there will always be someone else to blame. Isn't it just easier to pass the buck than to accept blame? It has got to be someone else's fault that the project is incomplete, that the client didn't receive the expected service that the relationship didn't work out, that the marriage failed, that he fell ill and the list is endless. The ego finds it much more easier to shift the blame onto another person rather than to accept blame. If you have to accept blame, it means you may need to humble yourself and accept what is happening in the present moment. The ego cannot survive in the present moment. It dies. How can it die? It will not allow that. So it makes it even more challenging for the human to accept blame. Once you accept blame, you apologise. You open yourself up. You become understanding. You become gentle and kind. You become your true self. You are your true self. Remember that your true self is pure and it will continue to show you that it exists, no matter how long it takes for you to realise, accept and embrace your true self, more and more things will happen in your life. The ego's destiny is to dissolve. So whichever way you look at, it, it is bound to happen. See it for what it is and you will realise what you are not.

The ego is addicted to inner conflict and torment. It needs you to be unhappy and dissatisfied. This is the pursuit of the ego. So for as long as you are miserable and for as long as you always have desire and fear and wants and needs, it will strengthen. It is associated to anything that is considered negative in your life. Be it a thought, a belief, an emotion or an action. If you have identified something as negative, you will immediately identify it as being associated to your ego, which seeks to destroy you at some point.

Look within to create without; I free myself from my Ego

By now, you have a need to get rid of this ego that you have become aware of. And the first question that enters your mind is how do I do this? I cannot destroy or master it, as this will strengthen it. Choose to become aware of it. Choose to become conscious of your true self. Focus on the positive light that is in you. You cannot focus on the ego and expect your true self to emanate its light. You must focus on your true self; strive towards finding your inner self and then bringing it to the surface.

By doing this, you will slowly find that the ego will self –destruct. It will diminish. It will dissolve. Whatever you place the most amount of energy and time on, will increase. For example, if I had to plant a rose seeds for a rose garden and every single day, I put a certain amount of my energy and time watering the garden, nurturing it, removing the weeds, talking to it and giving it all of my attention, the most beautiful roses will come to fruition. As a result of the energy that I gave to it, it will increase and grow and strengthen. Likewise for anything else in your life be it a positive or a negative thing, a good or a bad, as long as you give it attention, it will become more of itself. So I am not asking you to focus on your ego. I have asked that you are conscious and aware of it. Turn your attention and your energy unto yourself. Begin with emotional detachment from all external material objects. Move towards your own inner light. Understand that you are valuable. God has created you magnificently. He did not say you would become magnificent only once you attain wealth and status. He loves you and approves of you with no bearing on your appearance, possessions or career. He loves you through your good and bad deeds and this is why we know God to have characteristics of forgiveness, mercy and abundance. Many people believe that if they have been a bad person who is ego-centred, who has hurt others, who has wronged others or sinned against God, they believe that there is no hope for them. So instead of rectifying their flaws and starting a new leaf, they despise themselves. They are unsatisfied with actions from the past that tend to hold them captive and control them. So they continue on their journey of faults and flaws. They have not forgiven themselves, and by not doing so, there is lack of self-acceptance. Instead there is guilt, shame, embarrassment and no improvement. These emotions do not serve you and these thoughts do not add any value to your life. In fact, all that has happened is that you became aware of your ego, your identified and admitted to your faults but you still feel and think like a victim. Which means that the ego is still very much alive. You may not harm or hurt others but you are hurting yourself. So the cycle will continue and experiences from your past will occur repeatedly, just with different people, different timing and different experiences. The same emotions, self-humiliation and need to receive pain or inflict hurt on others will continue. First you show them your best face. You impress them, you are true to yourself and your virtues of kindness, love, compassion and endurance reflect. As time passes, so to does your virtues and once again, the ego will surface and along with it comes pain, desire, fear and resentment.

Life will present itself with many blessings. You will open up a new business. You may qualify as a surgeon. You may inherit huge sums of wealth from a deceased family member. Life is full of surprises. When you least expect something to happen, something really bold will happen. And most of the time, it is something truly amazing. When it does happen, in your heart, you will know that everything bad that has ever happened to you in your life brought you to this moment of bliss. You will tend to let go of things that may have hurt you. You may smile in the face of your good news with acceptance and humility. Within us all, there is both positive and negative. If you think that you can go through life wanting only the good, you are delusional.

There is no pain without pleasure. These are 2 sides of the same coin. However, we as humans have been blessed with choice.

For as long as you are blessed with choice, you are accountable and responsible for your own life that you create. If you have the ability to choose, then the consequences of your choice will be what life will present to you on a platter. The first place that you could ever begin to make changes is within the confinement of your mind. Your mind is inside of you. It is internal. Not external. So no longer look outside, no longer look for answers in other people. Stop. Take some time to breath in deeply and care to look inside. You will be surprised that the answer to every question you could have ever asked yourself or will ever ask yourself, is in fact within you and it will surface. The answer must come. It cannot come until you look inside and ask.

Inside of you, there is beauty, peace, calmness, love, generosity, kind-heartedness, compassion, empathy, gentleness and purity. It is already within you. You do not have to acquire it. It is already there. You do not need to become it. It is already there. You just need to shed some light onto it. You do not have to do good deeds and thereby try to become good. That will be another ego identity. You have to find the goodness that is already within you.

Move your attention away from your desires, attachments and obsessions with the outer world. As humans, you cannot escape from the outer world; you must live in and with it. You cannot run from it. The more you want it, the further and faster away it will run from you. The more you focus on your inner self; you will attract wealth and success and perfect health in abundance because these are gifts to enjoy, not to obsess over and certainly not to become attached to.

As the ego diminishes, you will find that you do not need to make extra effort to impress anybody or even lie about anything. You will not need to go out of your way to prove your worth or value. It will happen effortlessly. You will gain respect and honour without much action on your side besides being true to yourself. Allowing your inner light to shine. You will no longer need a spotlight. You will not care for needing or wanting to be important or recognised or treated in a specific manner. It will happen on its own, without your interference. This is living your highest values. This is the death of the ego.

Self Help & Assessment Exercises

Chapter Four

Manage the Ego - Material Attachments

- Write down at least 6 of the possessions in your life that you believe are of great value to you and in the next column, write down how owning each possession makes you feel

List the item that you possess / own	How does owning this item make you feel about yourself
1.	

2.	
3.	
4.	
5.	
6.	

- Now, ask yourself & pen down your answers:

- If you were to not have any of the above possessions any longer in your life, how would it make you feel?

- Do you feel as if you may lose the respect and acknowledgement that you currently receive from friends, family & colleagues?

- Will losing the above items, cause you to lose your self-esteem or create a lack of self-acceptance for you?

- From your 6 possessions listed above, write down at least 3 items that you consider as most valuable to you.

- You now have a list of 6 possessions that are less valuable to you. Make an attempt to choose one of those possessions and give it away to someone.

- If you are able to give that item away to someone, you have managed to detach yourself from not just that specific object but you have detached yourself emotionally and mentally where you no longer need to identify your worth through that material object.

- This may seem like a trivial exercise to you, however you will realise the significance of this action and the positive impact it will have in your life.

- Write down at least 3 possessions that you think you may speak about in a conversation and one reason why you think you need to mention what you own, when speaking to someone else.

-

Item	The reason you think you need to mention what you own
1.	
2.	
3.	

- Now, ask yourself & pen down your answers:

- If you do not mention any of the above possessions in any work or personally related conversation, do you feel that the other person will still remain interested in your worth and value?

- Do you think you would be able to hold a conversation whereby you will not mention any of the things that you own?

Self – Help Exercise – Your sense of self

- How often do you think you use the following words in a day My, Mine and I

- Describe your reaction (thoughts, words, actions, behaviour) when you find yourself in an argument with someone you care about, work with, friends or family, especially if you think you are correct and the other party thinks otherwise

- Are you someone who would choose to remain silent or voice your opinion?

- If so, write down a typical example of your behaviour, words and actions when you were in such a situation.

- Write down what is the worst thing that could happen to you, should you be defeated in the argument

The next time you find yourself in such a situation, remember to ask yourself the following:

- Will I diminish if I choose to remain silent rather than argue and fight?
- Will I stop loving and accepting myself?
- Do I wish to be right to feed my ego and will this make me feel better?

What am I going to accomplish by fighting back / arguing / proving / justifying in that specific moment

Is there no better time to get my message across by using alternate methods of communication?

How am I feeling right now? Will I be speaking from a place of neutrality or are there emotions involved?

What am I going to lose and what am I going to gain from this argument?

- Take 10 minutes out of your day to isolate yourself from everyone in a quiet space.
- Remove all make-up, perfume, jewellery and anything that you may be wearing that is an external material object including earrings, watches and even branded clothing.
- Put on a simple, comfortable, unlabelled outfit.
- Now, for 10 minutes, close your eyes and sit in silence and in stillness, in a state of meditation where you will connect directly with your Creator, free of all thought, free of yourself, free of your mind. Just be a humble, ordinary human being in isolation. You may want to practise breathing techniques and other ways of meditation but here, you are acknowledging your true self and allowing yourself to be in a state of complete nothingness, free of the ego.
- I have included meditation techniques at the back of the book for you to practise.
- The lesson here is to realise that you have the ability to detach yourself emotionally,

physically and mentally from external objects and people and situations in your life without having to feed your ego but instead, you will choose to be true to yourself and still have everything that you want

Chapter Five

Be the Authentic You

"There is only one you in this entire Universe. That is the most amazing gift so be true to yourself"

Successful Leader Interview

Mr Muhammad Ra'id (Rushen) Naidu

CEO, South African Business Support Centre

Tell us a little more about your humble beginnings?

I worked for my father as a cashier, a driver and other areas of his business from a young age. Although, I come from a well-established family, my father has taught me the importance of achieving your own goals and working towards your own achievements in life. He has been an inspiration to me. Based on this, I opened my first company in 2007 in the electronics and IT industry. This company was run successfully, and had a staff complement of 60. I then ventured into other areas of business. Today, I run 2 companies namely South African Business Support Centre as well as MTS Travel Specialists. I have a vision and will continue to strive towards wealth and success by setting and achieving goals one at a time.

What is your definition of success?

Success is the ability to touch people's hearts and assist them to achieve their own dreams. In this way, I believe that my own success is created. It is having the art of giving without expectation of anything in return. Success is not based on monetary or material value, rather it is, more about doing for others and at the same time, you will find that God takes care of your needs without your interference.

What makes you a leader?

I have the gift of understanding people and identifying their needs. I am also able to determine the potential in people and help them embrace their worth and unique talents and maximise on opportunities to create and fulfil their own goals. Leadership is to be an example and not hold onto a title of who you think you are. Also, I value what my clients say about me. I prefer listening rather than talking.

What advice do you have to offer young aspiring entrepreneurs?

Realise your true worth and your true potential. Focus on contributing towards the greater good for everyone and not just yourself. Work from a humble foundation and always ensure that your intentions are sincere. Do not expect results now. Anything that you want and receive now, cannot last. Be prepared for the long haul and trust that it will all be worth your effort and dedication.

What kind of mind-set do you have? Tell us a little more about your thoughts and how they affect your life?

My mind-set is based on the 5 pillars of Islam, which are Kalimah (Belief in the Oneness of God), Salaah (prayer), Zakaah (Charity), Fasting & Hajj (Pilgrimage to the Holy Land). I have chosen to follow the teachings and example of the Beloved Prophet Muhammad (Peace Be Upon Him).

His teachings and way of life is all the mentorship and coaching that I require in all aspects of my life be it finance, personal or health. I think that honesty, sincerity, humility and transparency are foundations that have allowed me to accomplish my goals and pioneer towards success.

Life is a journey and an amazing experience. We should allow ourselves to focus more on the positive and free our minds from that which we perceive as negative as God does not put any situation into our lives whatsoever, unless there is something we can benefit from it.

Value your Originality

God ordained your existence. You were born out of His Divine Order. You are unique and beautiful and special in more ways than one. Let's go back to when we were children. As very young children, we were accepted and loved even when we were not on our best behaviour. We entered the world with confidence and trust in God that we will be cared for and that provision will be made available for our survival. Life continued and we are grown into adulthood. Yet as adults, we find faults within ourselves.

When I was younger, I had a burning passion within me to achieve. I was not quite sure what it is I wanted to achieve. All I knew was I wanted to achieve something in life. I wanted to become somebody. I wanted to be different. After matric, I studied here and there from hotel management to journalism, tourism, travel and anything that I found a sudden interest in. I enjoy speaking to people. When I speak to people, it gives me feel good emotions. So as years passed, I moved from one job opportunity to another in pursuit of achievement. Still, uncertain of what it is exactly I wanted to achieve. The search continued for many years until I eventually opened up my own company three years ago. And I thought to myself: "I have achieved my goal but, was this what I wanted?" I still felt a void inside of me. I felt somewhat unfulfilled.

Along the timeline of my life, there were many, many successful people that I admired. I wanted to be more like them. Perhaps if I behaved or spoke like them, I would become like them. Perhaps, if I took on a different personality or character, I would be better equipped to achieve something. And through this search for fulfilment and achievement, I had experienced emotional breakdowns, lack of self-worth, and an uninspiring marriage and even became a mother at the age of 22.

When I had my daughter, I thought to myself. Wow, well isn't that an achievement. She is precious to me and I love her dearly but it wasn't really the "achievement"

Around the age of 24, I decided to drop all masks. I wanted to be myself. I made a conscious decision to value my originality and that means doing things that made me happy, behaving in a manner I was comfortable with, no matter who was around me. Being absolutely original and true to myself.

Of course, by now, all those people who didn't like my originality were removed from my life by the course of nature and all those who walked into my life, valued my originality.

So I want to know from you, what is originality? How can we define being an original person?

It is to have one personality throughout your life. It is to be a consistent human being in your thoughts, beliefs, actions and behaviour. And when I say consistent, I am not saying that you are not allowed to change your mind about things in life. Life evolves. Humans evolve. Evolution is part of our existence. So change will happen. Being consistent does not affect our evolution. Our values and our morals will streamline through all changes in our lives. I am a presenter on radio on the weekends. I present a show where I explore all places of interest, holiday destinations, activities and travelling information to listeners. I interview activity owners, give away some awesome vouchers and we have lots of fun on air. People call into the show and it is a show that people have become accustomed to on a Sunday afternoon. Recently, when my grandmother fell ill, there had been lots of visitors to the home. Some far related family had come through to see her and there was this lady who said to me "Aren't you the presenter of this show on radio?" to which I replied with a smile "Yes, I am. And thank you for listening" She then went onto say "Well I must tell you that I am at home all day and I listen to this particular radio station all day and I am familiar with every presenter but from everyone that speaks on air, you are the most original" At first I didn't understand what she meant so I asked her to please explain. She went on to say that it was easy for her to relate to my words and me because I sounded very real. I did not sound as if I adopted an accent and neither did I speak in a way that normally seems like "an act" as those were her words, not mine. She summed it up beautifully as being original. I was humbled by her comments and agreed to the fact that I had been true to myself. I didn't care to be like or sound like anyone else, I chose to be me. And whether you accept me or dislike me for my originality, I have no control over that. The only thing that I can control is myself. So be it on or off air, the conversation, and I, will be exactly the same.

If you think that actors only exist in movies, you are mistaken. Do you know how many people there are out there that have the potential to be the best actors you would ever meet in your life? People joke about it all the time "You should win an Oscar for that" they would say to someone.

When you are acting, you are assuming a role and through that becoming that which you are not. So, when you engage in business, social networks or with your family and friends, you tend to adopt different personalities and behaviour dependent on the situation that you are in. The majority of people will agree that there is no harm in assuming a role when placed in a position where it is required of you. But, the challenge arrives when you have assumed so many different roles and personalities in your external engagements that the chances of playing the wrong role with the wrong person may surface sooner or later. It is quite difficult to keep up with yourself if you are not authentic and true to yourself. I have been introduced to the likes of several personalities. A businessman I met once comes to mind. He assumes the role of a wealthy, dynamic and successful businessman when he is attending high profile events and rubbing shoulders with like-minded people. Note that I said like-minded people. He will don his best suit, perfume and appearance to ensure that he meets the criteria of the event. He will walk in an upright manner, speak with proficiency, use words that he does not necessarily know the meaning of and interact with others representing himself in the manner that he needs people to "buy".

And this very same person is a totally different person at home, where he is humble, shy and conservative. He doesn't care much about his sense of dressing and neither does he care to impress anyone. These are contradictory personalities. However we must understand that he has a professional face and a home face. So naturally, he will assume the roles accordingly.

What happens in the instance where you happen to meet the same crowd of people at a business meeting as well as at an informal social gathering? What if you have no choice but to take off your mask? Perhaps you might have said something really outstanding about yourself at the formal event or spoke about a specific achievement or accomplishment and maybe you exaggerated the story a bit. And then at the informal gathering, the topic comes up and the truth is revealed. Again, the ego plays its role here. You will need to become someone you are not.

Do not be mistaken. There is a difference between being professional and being egocentric. There is a difference between being well groomed and boasting about your achievements. There is a difference between being well spoken and lying. There is no harm in being a diligent, professional, smart and well-spoken person. Who says you cannot be all of this, and maintain your originality? Without disregarding your authentic personality.

It is amazing how we drop all masks when we are with those whom we love and trust. Those people who make no judgements upon us. Those people who tolerate us and accept us. This is normally our immediate family and in many instances our friends. Here, we are original. We express ourselves sincerely, we say things that we mean and through that lose our pride, arrogance and attitude. The reason we are original around our friends and family is because we trust them. We feel safe in their company. We feel as if they make no judgements upon us and we make no judgements upon them. We are able to behave in a manner we are comfortable with, and it is a safe space for us to express our feelings, our thoughts and our true selves without having to look over our shoulders.

The flip side to this coin is; although you may think and feel safe with those whom you love and trust, you are bound to encounter an experience in your life where those that are closest to your heart, whom you have felt safest amongst, will be the very same people to judge you. After all, you let your guard down; you expressed your true original self, flaws and all. You have shown your weaknesses and at some stage, with at least one person in your life, you may find that they were the person you needed the most protection from. They expose your weaknesses, they play on your emotions and they even use your own originality to make you feel guilty or disappointed in yourself. It is this very experience that you learn from. Some people go through several of these experiences, not just one. They will continue to stumble across more and more people that they may choose to be authentic in front of and find out that they have been deceived at a later stage. And as time goes by, you no longer wish to expose your original selves. You become protective of your true self. You guard your authenticity as if it were gold never to be exposed. This is why, especially in the world of business and even more so in close knit families, you will speak to someone and they will tell you just how much they dislike a certain someone else be it an employer, employee, colleague, friend or close relative. They will always complain about the person and have nothing positive to say about them. However, to your amazement, at the next function, you will see them smiling and laughing and enjoying a long conversation with that very same person.

As I was growing up, I witnessed this repeatedly and I could never understand what was going on. How does someone smile and eat and laugh with another person that they dislike? How is that ever possible? I am 27 years old and I can tell you now, that I still do not know how to do it. To me, it seems like you are cheating your true self. The famous saying goes "Keep your friends close and your enemies closer" well I am sorry but for me, that is the most difficult thing one could ever ask me to do. If I am not comfortable around you, you are bound to know. You will see it from the distance that I keep and from my body language that I am not willing to engage with you on any level. I choose to be true to my feelings and myself. This does not mean that we should go around harbouring any ill feeling against, or dislike for anyone. These patterns have been ingrained in us for so long, that it is difficult to simply cast them off. But cast them off we must. It will take time, but a willing heart will be a handy tool in the attempt.

So, you see, there are so many different definitions of being "original" and being "authentic"

At some stage in your life, you are going to have to expose your true self. And your true self is pure and beautiful. I will continue to repeat this throughout the book until you grasp this completely. Your true self is perfect; it is a place of trust and love. Give yourself permission to be an authentic human being. You only have one life in this world. You are aware that your soul will continue to live on, it is the self conscious mind and the body that dies, that departs from this world and enters the next realm of existence. We get this. However, you are allowed to live in this world. You must interact and engage with other human beings, animal and nature. It is part of existing.

At this point you may have realised that this seems to be a rehash of one of the points discussed in the last chapter on ego. If you do realise that, then you are correct. That's good, because it means you are getting the idea, you have begun to understand the ego and become aware of its function. This particular trait of the ego is extremely important as we face it daily in our interaction with others. We may be role-playing ourselves, or we may have witnessed others doing it, but becoming aware of it will guide us on how to deal with it. Becoming aware of it will be the start of the end of it. It is for this reason that I discuss it more detail.

Inconsistent Role Play

So the question is, why not interact authenticity? Why be afraid of your originality? Some time back, I had an acquaintance that would never be caught without make-up. Her identity and her sense of being were only evident through her make-up. There would never be a day in her life or even a night for that matter where she had no make-up on her face. And I am not talking about normal make up like a lipstick or eyeliner. I am talking about heavy make-up for every inch and feature of the face. It was impossible to ever imagine what this person looked like in her original form. What would she look like if she removed those false eyelashes? Would her face look different without that much of blush on her cheeks? Would she be a totally different person if she removed those hair extensions? My mine would always wander and try to picture this woman in her true original, authentic form. She was breathtakingly beautiful and her make up made her look like a doll, or like she'd just stepped out of a glossy fashion magazine.

But what was beneath that surface? Why was she so afraid to ever show her face without make up? And I am not saying that maybe it is because she is unattractive, no. In fact I would say that without make up she is probably even more stunning. This is not the answer at all. The point that I am trying to make is she had made a decision to not be true to her self, to not be original, to not be authentic perhaps it was a result of a broken heart or some mishap that she may have experienced in her life. So, she prefers to cover herself up with make up and dare not face the world without it. People must see what she wants them to see. Perhaps she is uncomfortable with herself and therefore she feels that others may not like her. Life makes people this way. People are not born making these decisions. Things happen and then you pull away from the world. You start protecting yourself. I want to emphasize the importance of your originality and authenticity. What would happen should this woman fall ill or experience old age in her life where she will need many people around her? What would be worse to her – the illness, old age or having to expose her true face to the world? To some, this may sound absurd, but if you can relate to this story, then go and try to wipe off all of your make-up and anything that you wear or have on you that is false. Remove it completely and then go out and face the world. Some people would never dare attempt this. There is fear. How can they expose their authentic self? Well, it is not a bad thing at all. It is not frightening and it can bring no harm into your life. In fact, if you make a decision to be authentic and true to yourself, you might even feel as if a heavy burden and responsibility has been lifted off your shoulder.

Another example is of a woman saying "I will never be caught dead without my high heels" This may seem vain and obnoxious but it is through her high heels that she derives her sense of self. It is through her high heels that she gains confidence and self-esteem; it is through external conditions and desires that she is able to find the good within herself. Does this seem foolish? Does this mean that without her heels, she loses her self-esteem? Does she lose her value if she walks around in flat shoes? Or is it that she becomes original and authentic without her heels. And she cannot allow others to see her in this way. They will only see what she wants them to see.

Priceless Authenticity

Being an original and authentic person does not mean that you need to only be true to your external physical self. It is not possible to make any changes to the outer self unless the inner self has been found. The first step to finding yourself is to lose yourself because you cannot find anything until it is has been lost.

What makes you happy? My answer to that would be chocolate. Chocolate makes me happy. But when the sugar rush is over, I experience an all-time low. Some people find happiness in food and others find happiness in people. Some find it in wealth and some find it in success.

You have heard the saying that the "Happiness comes from that which money cannot buy" and some may say, "Of course money will bring happiness. When you have money, you can buy whatever you want. If you have whatever you want, you will find happiness" Yet little do they realise that happiness cannot be found or gained externally. Yes, I agree that spending quality time with your loved ones or enjoying a meal with good company or purchasing something you have always wanted does bring about happiness in you. You identify the feeling of elation as happiness. You call it happiness. If you look deeper within yourself, in silence and in stillness, you will discover that happiness is the space inside of you that exists. This is a space of no thought and only positive feelings. It is the smallest encounter or act that could happen in someone's life that brings them happiness. Something that may be observed as unimportant or irrelevant is in fact the very reason for someone's happiness. It cannot be understood or defined with words, because it is felt in the heart.

There is absolutely nothing wrong with you. You are different. You are unique. There is no other person on the earth that can be compared to you. You are special to at least one other person in this world. And there is at least one other person that is special to you. You have a personality that cannot be compared to someone else's simply because you are who you are. Make a decision to accept yourself. And affirm, "I accept myself for who I am and I love myself and everything about me, I may not be a perfect human being, I make mistakes but that is okay. I will learn from my mistakes and I will grow and develop positively."

Not being perfect is excellent. In fact, who and what define perfection? Is there a certain law that says "This is the law of perfection and this is the criteria, if you do not meet the criteria, you are not perfect"?

Perfection cannot be defined because within perfection itself is flaws and faults. How would you identify something as perfect if you do not know what a mistake is? One cannot exist without the other. There is no need to be perfect. Rather, strive to be authentic and allow your authenticity to reflect from within.

Parents have played a fundamental role in our lives. It is from our parents that we have learnt more about life and developed our characters. Parents instil what they themselves have been taught, into their children. It is how the cycle of life has always been and most probably will continue to be unless there is a huge shift in consciousness.

As we were growing up, we were taught virtues and values. We were taught how to practice patience, how to be kind to others, how to respect people, how to speak, sit, eat and even walk. From childhood to adulthood, we have implemented the morals and values that have been taught to us by our parents, family and caregivers – those people who we trust and who love us unconditionally.

It's therefore irrelevant what level of education we achieve or how qualified we become for our true inheritance is that which we have learnt from our parents. Of course, each of us has had unique childhoods, raised by different types of parents. My parents are different from yours. You may be a parent and I am too. I have beliefs, ideologies and habits that are being observed by my curious 5-year-old daughter.

She seeks to emulate me by wanting to wear what I wear, telling me that she wishes to be just like me. And this humbles me and of course brings a smile to my face. To her, I am perfect but, to myself, I am imperfect. I accept that I have flaws and I am much more conscious and aware of my words and actions in her presence as I know she is like a sponge absorbing it all at this stage in her life.

For all of time, parents have disciplined their children in some way. Receiving discipline from our parents is how we learn the rules of life. Then there are adults, who today, are not only parents but also grandparents who have come from broken homes, abusive backgrounds, unsteady childhoods, confusion, emotional blackmail and a long possible list of circumstances. What children learn as children, they act upon as adults and then teach their children the very same thing – it is a cycle.

If you grew up in a broken home, were raised within an abusive situation, or even lived in poverty as a child, would you then allow the cycle to continue with your own children?

If you have been taught rules and regulations about life, finance, religion, beliefs, culture, health or work, did you just accept it all for what it implemented it without question? Or did you have the courage to question things that you were taught, have an enquiring mind and investigate it further before accepting it as true? The natural thing to do is to accept. In fact, it is the easiest thing to do. We trust our parents and my daughter trusts me. In no way, am I saying that parents have led us down the incorrect path or that we should not listen to them, because the wisdom and knowledge from we receive our parents are invaluable. We respect our parents and honour them for their efforts and contribution towards our lives. This goes without saying.

God has, however, blessed us with a mind and the power of choice. For example, if I come from a poor family, I do not believe that I will also be poor – poverty is not inherited. I believe that I create my own reality and if I choose wealth then I will work towards wealth. How will I do this? I will do this by truly thinking, believing, feeling and taking action to change my situation or circumstance.

People in the world are suffering. Really. They are suffering. They suffer from negative beliefs about life. If a parent told their child "Money is evil, we are better off without it, we are happier" or things like "Don't worry to study after school, you rather find a job and work. There are people today who studied and don't have jobs so don't waste your time studying, find a job and work"

Do they realise the seriousness and consequences of their teachings? Do they have any idea as to what mind-sets they are creating in their children? These young adults will listen. Firstly, what is the point of trying to do well in school and get good grades if I am not going to study further anyway? So once the school life is over, they find a job, earn a regular wage that may afford them a cell phone and airtime and some nice branded clothing perhaps and they continue to live with their parents and work for the rest of their lives. The occasional promotion, raise or slight move up the company ladder may occur, but nothing of great significance over a long period of time. And they are absolutely fine with this, they do not wish for more and, to them, studying is irrelevant.

There is no right or wrong. I am merely trying to shed light on the importance of not just accepting thoughts and beliefs in our lives but actually investigating further before embedding it into the sub-conscious mind. How is all of this relevant? Well let me explain.

As adults, because of evolving consciousness, we awaken to the truth. So whether it is a small or a big thing, there has to be something you will come across or realise that your parent would have taught you that you do not agree with and have a different opinion of. Or to be more specific, if you were abused or spoken to badly or screamed and shouted at, you may decide that you will not do the same to your children. But most people do. Those who say I will not be anything like my parent, in most cases, are exactly like their parent that they didn't want to be. It is not intentional. It is unconscious. You will find yourself doing something or saying something that you told yourself you would never ever do but it happens and you do it. Can we call this being original? Can we call this being authentic? I am not here to answer all the questions. I am just asking questions that only you can think about deeply and answer according to your own life experiences.

Just know that whatever we have been taught by our parents is what they have learnt from their elders. To a lot of the smart young adults today who know everything, there is a lot of fault finding in your parents. Accept that if they knew anything more than what they taught you, they would have taught it to you! So basically they have imparted knowledge and wisdom according to their own knowledge and wisdom. I do not know of any parent who would decide to teach you only half of what they know and keep the rest of this information be it good or bad, to themselves, as a secret.

When you learn to forgive your parents and accept them completely, your heart will soften to the fact that they were only doing the best that they could. And if they were abusive and insulting then understand that they were abused and insulted and therefore they carried out their behaviour accordingly. It does not condone their behaviour however at least you can understand why it happened.

Once you open your heart to the first mentors and leaders in your life – your parents - you will find it much easier to make a success of yourself, in your own life. Once you acknowledge that if there were things that you experienced that you did not like, you can forgive and let it go. Do not dwell on those thoughts and those emotions and those beliefs that you are holding onto. Sometimes, you will find that you still have a certain belief that you know, does not serve you and will not benefit your life however because it was drummed into your head all your life, you still carrying this belief with you and you will find that you keep stumbling on your path whenever you implement that belief or live it out. That stumbling is a sign to let go of it. Your heart and thoughts are yours. Nothing and nobody could ever have a hold or have control over how you should be or what they want you to be. Your authentic true self will always rise to the surface. Holding onto resentment or pain or feeling like a victim about the not so perfect life you might have lived cannot and will not improve your life in anyway whatsoever. Of course there are lessons to be learnt and you will learn them when the time is right. The lesson has always been there, always in front of you. You were just not conscious of it at the time. So every pain, every challenge, every difficulty that life has ever presented to us, even the parents that we are blessed with, whether they helped us or hurt us, has been and will always be for our own greater good.

Your life story will always be different to someone else's. Your problem will always be your problem. You can relate it to other people. But it is your experience to live through. Your dreams, visions and goals will always be yours to achieve. In business, in relationships, in any aspect of your life, it is yours. Again, it seems like I'm talking about the ego, doesn't it?

But seriously, the best thing you could ever do for yourself is being true to who you are. You do not need to behave or "put on" any sort of identity to please another person. As long as you are a conscious mind and you are aware of yourself and you are able to take control of your mind, life will always lead you to where you were always destined to be. You are just not there yet because of your limiting beliefs. You are not there yet because you are filled with ideas and expectations of what and who you should be, whose standards you need to live up to, which person you need to make happy and all other responsibility to everyone else but yourself. So what happens? You lose your originality. You become someone you are not. You assume roles and identifications that are not an honest reflection of yourself.

Your authenticity is priceless. It will always be.

Chapter Six

Implementing Your Values

""Don't be a victim of your history, be a Master of your Destiny"

Dr John Demartini

Successful Leader Interview

Mrs Sheritha Kumar

Protea Hotels KwaZulu-Natal – South Africa

Tell us a little more about your humble beginnings?

I started off with Protea Hotels as a banqueting co-ordinator. I then moved onto many different areas within the hotel industry. With dedication, patience, perseverance, faith, dedication, today I head up the complete sales portfolio for Protea Hotels in KwaZulu-Natal. It has been quite an inspiring journey as there were many times where I felt like giving up however it took strength and courage to steer ahead and remain focused assuring myself that giving up is not who I am. My purpose in life is never to give up but to face every obstacle with a smile and use it as a stepping-stone to the next level of accomplishment.

What is your definition of success?

Success is having the ability to put my daughter through her studies and have a supportive and ambitious husband who always understood my highest values.

Through support, love and encouragement, I am where I am today. Success is also empowering my team and motivating them to never give up but instead work on their weaknesses and increase their own strengths. And lastly, success is having the ability to live a balanced life where your family, your children and your business receive maximum attention and to feel fulfilled and happy in each aspect of your life.

What makes you a leader?

I am a woman who is confident, strong and committed to anything that I put my mind to. In my position and especially for the team that I lead, I know the importance of being an example rather than speaking about what I want from them. Leadership is about doing more than just saying. Being involved in my team and working with them has proved to be successful for me.

What advice do you have to offer young aspiring entrepreneurs?

Whatever you have always dreamt of doing, go out there and do it. There is absolutely nothing that is stopping you from achieving your goals and fulfilling your dreams.

What kind of mind-set do you have? Tell us a little more about your thoughts and how they affect your life?

My thoughts revolve around things that inspire me. My family inspire me. My work team inspire me. Anything that inspires me motivates me to push forward. Even on a bad day, I wake up out of bed with a purpose in mind - a purpose to make a difference, do something positive or different from what I did yesterday. I also understand that giving to others is the secret to receiving anything. Without giving, it is impossible to receive any sort of abundance in my life.

Your values are your benchmark

Every human has his or her own blueprint for success and achievement. No two people are alike. This can be easily understood as being unique. Each one of us has our own set of values that we live up to. A value is something that we do in our lives that gives us a sense of fulfilment. People's values differ according to their own standards and lifestyles. If you are finding it difficult to identify your values then take pen and paper and note down all of the things that you are currently doing in your life everyday, repeatedly without anyone having to give you a sort of reminder. For example, one would say I go to work and I focus on my business all day. I come home. Spend some time with my family and then back to my work and business matters until late at night" Based on the things that you do most often, and may seem almost like an addiction and a passion, this is how you will identify your highest values. A value can also be noted as a high priority. It is something that you love, something that you feel committed to and something that you will continue to do no matter what anyone else thinks or says. Many people go through life without acknowledging their own values instead they choose to adopt the values of other people in their lives like a spouse, a parent or even an employer.

When you no longer focus on things that matter the most to you, you will find yourself living in the shadow of someone else who you may look up to. You feel as if their values are higher than yours and feel it is best if you adopt theirs and diminish yours. For those who adopt the values of others, there will always exist a level of dissatisfaction within themselves. For them, there will always be a sense of something lacking or feeling of being incomplete.

If you are in a relationship, you will find yourself doing things to make the other person happy. If you do not eat popcorn, you will find yourself eating popcorn to please your partner. Some situations are slightly more complex whereby one partner is obsessed with work and making money and the other is more focused on children and health. And sometimes, they clash as they find it challenging to co-exist, as their values are not the same. As a result, there are arguments, complaints and dissatisfaction from both partners. This is unhealthy for any relationship. However, if you begin to understand the significance of values and just how unique it is to every human being, it will be easier to co-exist with your partner or even a business partner out of respect for their own values.

When I said no two people are the same, I meant that of course without doubt; your partner's values will differ from yours. He or she is his or her own individual. If the both of you had to have the exact same values then one of you won't be needed in the relationship! So when I say to you that you need to identify and acknowledge your own values, I am also saying that once you do that, you have the ability to respect and accept the values of your partner. In this way, both of you will be living up to those things that mean the most to you, you will understand each other and improve the relationship from that point.

You might find that as much as your spouse loves and cares and provides for you, he holds his parents as his highest value or more specifically his mother. And, as his partner you may feel neglected, as though he pays her more attention than you. You will begin to complain and nag him about it because you do not accept his highest value. You, on the other hand, hold quiet time and the ability to read a good book in peace and quiet in high regard. Just because these two contrasting values exist, does not mean they negate or condone each other. They merely exist, need to be accepted as they are and respected.

Communicating about the things that mean very much to you is significant. If it is important to you, do not be in denial about it, because there is no need to deny what it is you value most. Perhaps you are denying it because you want to avoid an argument?

Would you really deny your highest value in order to avoid conflict? Your actions will always speak for themselves - it is not always what you say that is true, it is what you do. Through your actions, your values are apparent and you do not need to be reminded of them.

Let's look at a possible solution with the above scenario. Perhaps you can suggest that when your partner needs to take his mother shopping and you are not up for it, you could take the children and spend time at the park and carry your books along. In this way, you both are getting to do what you enjoy doing. There is understanding. In order for a relationship to sustain itself, it cannot happen if one person has to continuously diminish their values in order to keep up with the next person's one. Even if this were to happen, at some point, there will be crumbling. There will be exposure. The frustration and the anger will surface. Where you feel like you have had enough of doing what you don't enjoy and your resentment and long standing silence leaves you with no choice but to vent. This is far worse of a situation to deal with. Balance plays a very important role in any type of relationship. Understanding the importance of doing things that make you feel fulfilled and satisfied paves way for the timeline of goals that eventually lead to your ultimate vision.

People around the world are stuck doing jobs that they do not like yet because it provides an income and sustainability, they will remain stuck in that job. So although they are living their values that is working and providing for their family, they are not necessarily satisfied. In fact they are miserable. They are doing something that does not fulfil their true purpose. And if you do anything that does not fulfil your true purpose in life, you will always feel incomplete and unsatisfied no matter how great the salary or lifestyle may be.

The best way to identify your values is to write down things that you love to do and enjoy doing. Make a detailed list of all of the things that you are passionate about. When you are younger, you adopted a hobby. As people grow into adults, they let go of their hobby because they have other commitments and responsibilities that leave no time for them to fulfil their hobby. But it is the hobby that gave them the sense of satisfaction and feel good emotions. It is only the things that you enjoy in life that will ever give you the fulfilment that you seek.

A few years ago, I was sitting in a hotel restaurant enjoying lunch with the general manager of the hotel. We got into discussion about what matters most to each of us in our own lives and she mentioned that her dream was to always own a beauty parlour. She was fascinated with hair, make-up, acrylic nails and everything that beautifies a woman. In fact, in her spare time, she was at the beauty parlour enjoying all of these things. She said that she enjoyed managing a hotel and paying attention to guests was at the top of her priority list but it was not her true purpose and passion. Her job as the general manager was there for her to provide an income and meet the monthly expenses. So, I told her to get up, we were going somewhere. She was curious. I took her to a nearby place where I had known the owner of a shop which was in fact a fully kitted out beauty parlour. The owner had invested large sums of money into creating a modern and beautiful beauty parlour however he had no skilled staff to run the business and he looked for someone to take it over. Immediately, they connected. She opened up the parlour, employed staff and a manager and it turned into a thriving business. She maintained her job in the hotel however she spent her weekends and evenings at the parlour engaging with clients and fulfilling her true purpose.

It is when this happened that she found a sense of completeness. She realised that in order for her to feel completely satisfied and aligned to her true highest values, she would have to pursue it. A simple conversation over lunch had changed her life.

If you are currently in a situation where you feel as if you have not figured out your purpose as yet, do not despair. You are completely sane and everything is going to be perfectly fine. You could be a waiter, a housekeeper, a beautician, a teacher or even a student. You are working in a job doing what you are doing because it provides an income. It does not fulfil your true purpose. You feel hopeless right? Well let's change that. How about you review the list I asked you to write earlier.

If you have a list of ten things that you love to do, remove items from that list that are least important to you and identify the top 5 things that you love to do. And then ask yourself in what possible way can you achieve that specific value? There could be something on your list that you may think will not bring you income but I can assure you that if you identify your true purpose and you are good at it, you will definitely be able to make money from it. As the famous saying goes "Do what you love and you will never work a day in your life"?

Let me give you a few examples:

A woman works as a revenue manager in an international hotel group. She is outstanding in her job. In fact she is brilliant and admired by her peers. She earns a comfortable salary and she has been working this job for years. However she does not feel fulfilled or complete in her job. So I asked her once, what is your passion? What do you love and enjoy doing? She says she loves baking birthday cakes for children. She went on to follow her passion and baked gorgeous animated birthday cakes for children. Soon, more and more people fell in love with her creation and are keen to pay her to make birthday cakes for their children. Today, she works her day job, fulfils her highest value and experiences immense joy and satisfaction in creating the most colourful, prettiest and tastiest birthday cakes. And, she earns money from doing that which she loves.

So you see, it is possible. Anything is possible. Fulfilling your values is a very important aspect in your life. Why are you living if you are not living with a feeling of satisfaction and completeness? As I said, God has uniquely created you. You have a name and a surname. You can either choose to survive in this world and wait until you leave the world or you can search for your true purpose and identify your highest values and fulfil them. Leaving a legacy does not necessarily mean owning a successful business, being a wealthy man and leaving millions for your children to inherit. Leaving a legacy is where long after you are gone, people remember you. People still talk about you and how you have changed their lives in some way or the other. It doesn't even need to be some dramatic act or massive undertaking. It could be as simple as remembering how well you cooked, or as complex as having been a great surgeon. Leaving a legacy does not necessarily have to be linked to wealth, but if you are doing something in your life with passion, purpose and fulfilment, the chances of you earning an excellent amount of money are quite high.

So today, you are going to identify your highest values. By this I mean, you will define your list even further and turn them into your goals. We have short and long term goals. If a goal is long term, it becomes a vision. A vision is something that we identify as the end purpose, where we see ourselves at the end of the road, the thoughts, beliefs and emotions attached to what we can see in the distance when we look at our lives. That is a vision, a true purpose and fulfilment. I am not asking you to achieve your true purpose immediately, because your journey towards it will unveil all the intricacies of your true purpose along the way.

If there is something you feel will complete you or bring you satisfaction, you do not want or need immediate gratification. That is impulsive thinking where you decide that you wish to be a chef, for example, and seek out an opportunity to do just that. It does not work that way. If that is what you want, if that is your end thought in mind then you know that it is something you will aspire towards. The best way to get closer to your vision is to set goals for yourself. These goals become your benchmark. Everything is a process. You cannot get to your destination if you have not travelled through the journey and especially if you did not take all of the resources with you on the trip.

Let us make better sense of the way forward for you. Firstly you will make a list of everything that you love doing and then define that list further. You then need to set short-term goals for yourself and work towards achieving goal number 1. If you set 10 short term goals which will ultimately take you to vision and true purpose, you will become exhausted just looking at the list of goals and you may say to yourself "Well it seems quite impossible and a long road ahead, I don't know if I can forge ahead, maybe I should stick to what I am doing" This is absolute negative thinking. If it takes 5 years to reach your ultimate vision, and the goals are set out on a timeline over a 5 year period, you may feel well 5 years is a long time, leave it out, I cannot wait that long. And then you decide not to pursue it. However you are sabotaging yourself with that sort of thinking. Because when 5 years have passed, you will realise that you are in the same position and in fact it is 5 years later this is when you say to yourself "If I did pursue my goals, I would have reached my true purpose today" you will be exactly where you were 5 years ago as a result of your limiting beliefs.

So do not be controlled by the negativity of your mind. The self-conscious mind will never be short of reasons and excuses as to why you cannot achieve something that your heart is set out to do. If you do not take control and understand that unless you do something about it, nothing will happen and nothing will change. The thoughts in your mind will change, but the outer world will remain the same. Time will pass by, you will age and you will resent yourself even more for not doing something when you knew you had to do it. Forget about the long list of goals and don't pay much attention to the timeline. Just focus all of your attention on the first goal that needs to be achieved. For example, if you want to become a chef, the first thing you will do is research. So your first goal will be to research the various study courses and training schools that you will need to consider. Focus only on the first goal and do not worry about the goals that come thereafter. Those goals will become your focus naturally after you have achieved the preceding ones/

Maybe the first goal will be slightly different. If you want to become a chef yet you do not have funds to study the relevant courses, so your first goal will be to volunteer your services in your spare time to a restaurant in a hotel or in a shopping mall for that matter. Here you will work in the kitchen, learn from the professionals and have the opportunity to cook. So that would be goal number one - gaining experience by offering voluntary service in your spare time. Goal number two would be to start saving money and researching the study courses or training programmes that are available. And through your newly found network of restaurant personnel, you may receive better insight and information that will assist you in pursuing your next goal.

From there, your goals will become your benchmarks. No matter how big or small the goal is, the fact that you are aspiring towards achieving it and that your mind is focused on it, and when your thoughts, beliefs and emotions are equally aligned towards that goal, it is only a matter of time before it is achieved. Whatever you pay attention to and focus your energy on, will come to fruition.

Before you know it, your will reach your ultimate vision. You will find your true purpose and you will live a life of fulfilment and satisfaction. Nothing is stopping you from living that life right now. In fact you do not have to wait for the day to achieve your ultimate vision to be satisfied or fulfilled. Just by taking time off right now in your life to identify your highest values and make a conscious decision to work towards them, you will experience immense feelings of satisfaction and fulfilment by starting the process. By aspiring towards it. And as you progress along the timeline of your goals, that feeling will continue to increase. The first step before all else is to be grateful. Be appreciative of your current job, your present moment and all that it offers you because without it, you would not have realised what your highest values are. Without it, you may not have ever searched for anything more or a greater purpose.

Inspire Yourself Through Yourself

Through all goal setting and vision and value identification you undertake, make certain that your mind is in your control. There will be an abundance of negative thinking that will rise to the surface especially now that you have made a decision. Fear and ego will also come in the way of your goals and vision. Several thoughts will attempt to swallow and drown you so that you not pursue. You may even feel demotivated or despondent soon after you make your list of goals. This is where your true self must emerge. This is where you determination, commitment and endurance come into play. You must choose to not be overpowered by the thoughts in your mind that do not serve you. You must also be fully aware that your future is a blank piece of white paper with absolutely nothing on it. The picture that will be painted onto that white paper will be painted by your sub-conscious mind. And the sub-conscious mind takes instructions from your conscious mind. It is an obedient faithful servant to the self-conscious mind. And the self-conscious mind is dominated by ego and fear and endless thoughts of positive and negative alike. And then there is your true self; you super conscious self who is the ultimate master. That is you. You are the captain of the ship, you lead and everything thereafter will follow and manifest as your reality.

Motivation is a symptom. Over the years, I have attended several workshops on inspiration and motivation and positive thinking. I have also read books upon books about life, finance, relationships and it seems every single workshop and every single book makes a promise to you that it will change your life. And soon after you have attended the workshop or read the book, you will find yourself totally motivated. You will return to your workplace, business, relationship or home with a high-energy vibration of positivity and faith that your life has changed completely and you are a brand new person. Give it a few weeks, for some, even a month. You will notice that the person has fallen back into their old pattern of thought, he has become complacent and the motivation is gone. It disappeared. And if you have to ask him "Hey, what happened? Last month you were full of energy, you had such awesome plans for yourself and today you are back to your old self. You look demotivated, what is the matter? " And the response is not surprising. "Oh well, life happens. I have accounts to pay, a family to feed and lots of problems. I cannot be motivated, I have other things that need my attention right now"

How totally absurd does this sound. You are no longer motivated because life happened. And you would say that the book did not change your life. The workshop did not change your life. You blame everything external as "been there, done that, its just a strategy, it doesn't work" as your excuse or your reason simply because you did not make enough effort to make that change and stay motivated.

The only way you can stay motivated is if you consciously and confidently find more and more ways everyday of your life to inspire yourself through yourself. Nobody else can do this for you. Others can motivate you. They can share their own experiences, insights and secrets with you but unless and until, you decide that you hold the answers to every question in your life and it is only through you, that you can create something more true and inspiring for your greater good.

If you want to achieve anything in your life, if you are seeking your true purpose and have identified your goals and vision, understand that you do not need motivation. Motivation won't last. Look within yourself for ways in which you can inspire yourself.

Convince yourself that each step you are taking in your life will prove to give you fulfilment and enlightenment.

Losing all Judgement

To learn how to lose all judgement, we must understand why we judge. In order to do this, we have to look at the ego again. The most popular characteristic of the ego is something called criticism. Criticism is having the ability to look for faults in other people. The easiest way to divert attention from oneself is to criticise another human being. Try it. You will find out this truth for yourself. It is almost as if criticising a person is part of each human's identity. The funny part it is only humans that do it. I have never seen a flower finding fault in a slightly shorter or withering flower that stands beside it. In fact you will see the both of them swaying from side to side in harmony and perfection and in total acceptance of their value. Or even an animal for that matter, have you been told about the horse that gossiped to his mate about the sheep on the very same farm they lived on. This all sounds too absurd doesn't it?

Well, absurd it most certainly is! Humans have the ability within themselves to identify something that they feel or think is inappropriate in another thing or person. So let me ask you a question, if I introduce you to a Chinese man and he is speaking to you in the foreign language of Chinese. Besides just speaking, he is openly insulting you yet you do not understand the language of

Chinese right. So no matter how much he says or however insulting it may be, you will not be able to relate to his words because you do not understand it. The reason you do not understand it is because it does not exist within you. The Chinese language is not something that you have learnt. So in essence, we can conclude that unless something exists within you and you are familiar with it, you will not have the capacity or understanding to identify it in another person or thing externally.

How is it then that we are very quick to judge another human being? Let me give you a few examples:

- "Sarah is the most obnoxious and rude woman I have ever had to work with. She is self-centred and she loves attention!"
- "Mr Reddy is lying! Do not believe him. I know that he is lying. He has a habit of speaking lies"
- "My friend Jonathan cannot be trusted. I know he is my friend but if I were you, I would not trust him"
- "Who does she think she is? I bet you that it isn't even her money that she is spending. She probably has a wealthy boyfriend who bought it for her"

How harsh does this all sound? To me, it is filled with criticism and judgement of another person.

On the same token, I am saying to you that the only way you would have the capacity to identify these qualities and make such bold statements about anything or anyone is if unless of course, it exists within you. Or at some point in your life, you have done it. If it does not exist within you, if you cannot identify with it and if you have never done it before, it would be impossible for you to recognise it in somebody else. So lets further dissect these judgements.

This is what you are probably truly implying when you make such statements:

- "Sarah is the most obnoxious and rude woman I have ever had to work with. She is self-centred and she loves attention!"

Some part of me actually wishes it could receive the amount of attention that Sarah is receiving. There is self-centredness in myself as much as there is in Sarah. I have also been rude and obnoxious to other people.

- "Mr Reddy is lying! Do not believe him. I know that he is lying. He has a habit of speaking lies"

I have lied before in my life. I have not just lied once. I have lied quite a few times. This is why I am able to relate to Mr Reddy and his lies and because I know how to lie, I am able to identify that he is lying.

- "My friend Jonathan cannot be trusted. I know he is my friend but if I were you, I would not trust him"

I have broken someone's trust in my life. I may have even broken a friends trust. I know the feeling and the thoughts associated to breaking trust and I can easily relate to the fact that Jonathan cannot be trusted. I am letting you know this as well because I am familiar with this.

- "Who does she think she is? I bet you that it isn't even her money that she is spending. She probably has a wealthy boyfriend who bought it for her"

Maybe she is actually making her own money. I wish I had a wealthy boyfriend who could spoil me so that I can also behave in that manner. Or I would like to make that much money so that I can spend just as she is spending and enjoying.

Can you see the explanation for each statement? You may have told someone in your life at some point, "You are so gullible" or "You are so naive" if they cannot see a certain situation as clearly as you can. You may wonder to yourself "how stupid is she? It is so obvious but she cannot see it. She is so gullible" Well the truth is the reason she cannot "see" what you are seeing is because she cannot relate to it, she cannot relate to it because she cannot understand it because it is highly likely that those things that you want or need her to see does not exist within her. You may try to "open her eyes" or her mind however as long as she has not actually thought those very same thoughts or behaved in a similar way, it will be quite difficult for you to convince her. To me this makes perfect sense. What is within you, you will identify in the world around you.

How many people are living their lives criticising and judging others, making their own conclusions about other people's lives or businesses based on their own mind and their own qualities and values.

They impose their beliefs on an external situation where there is no truth. Just judgement. Anything outside of your soul and your body is a mirror and a reflection of what exists within your heart. Once you accept this and understand this, you will become conscious of your thoughts and you will become less critical and less judgemental of other people.

When you lose judgement, you have dissolved a very big part of the ego that exists in you. The ego loses its power and its strength. When you lose judgement, you will see the world with brand new eyes. It is zero based thinking. It is thoughts of beauty, love, kindness and generosity to name a few.

You will have the ability to understand people. You will be able to love everyone and accept everyone for who they are. You will be able to respect the values and priorities of other people that you engage with. You will begin to only think positive thoughts and become more aware of negative thoughts because you no longer have the desire to look for faults in other people but you accept them for what they are in front of you. There is no suspicion. There is no gossip. There is no criticism.

The next time you feel the urge to speak ill of your business partner, colleague, spouse or best friend, stop and say to yourself. Whatever I will say now is in fact a mirror and reflection of the type of person I am and these qualities exist within me as well" You may choose to be silent and keep your opinion to yourself or even better, you may change your opinion of that person and lose all judgement.

In order to thrive in your life and be successful and maintain your achievements, you must have within you the ability to celebrate and compliment the successes and achievements of other people. You must cease to be the person to find faults and make judgements upon another human being because you do not know them well enough to know if it is true. You will never be able to know anyone well enough because if you did, then you would be able to understand them instead of judge them. If you want to create success and wealth in your life, begin with zero based thinking. Energy flows where attention goes. By now, you may have discovered the significance of thoughts and the role that it plays in your life. It is thoughts that control your entire life and the way your life will unfold.

Thinking is something that happens to us. We do not choose to think, much like we do not actively think about breathing or digesting your food. Tell your children you need a moment to digest your food and, in just the same way, to think.

Thoughts will enter your mind from every direction you look. However your control is where you decide which thoughts to keep and which you release. Once that happens, you move onto forwarding the thoughts that serve you through to the sub-conscious mind and the rest is the manifestation to bring your reality to you. It is as simple as that.

So if you choose thoughts of criticism and judgement, you are creating a discouraging situation for yourself. Every thing you think, believe, feel or do has an effect on your reality called life no matter which way you look at it. Therefore you are responsible and accountable for your own life. Therefore the blame game will never work no matter how long in your life you choose to play that game. What you want to see happen in the world must first happen in you.

We are all made up of energy vibrating at different frequencies. Depending on the negative or positive energy of our thought, we will attract people vibrating at the same frequency. So when you are frustrated, you will always be meeting frustrated people. When you are kind and good to people, you will meet people that are kind and good to you. Do you think it is a co-incidence when people meet into an accident? They energy was vibrating at the same levels and they attracted each other into that situation. However, if you consciously decide that becoming a positive person, a less judgemental person and a more valuable person, all negative people that surround you will automatically disappear from your radar. All the things that made you unhappy or miserable will no longer exist. Those people and situations will move onto another level of energy frequency to more like-minded people.

Living up to your highest values including knowing that you have been put in this world to fulfil your true purpose and for you to search until you find that true purpose. Life will continue to put experiences in your lap until you get to that state of mind. You must be receptive and open to the idea of attaining and fulfilling your purpose. If you are closed to the Universe and if your mind rejects all new ideas and possibilities, you cannot go anywhere further from here. You will always remain where you are. Mentally. Emotionally. Physically. You must want to change. You must want to make a difference. You must want to search within yourself and the beauty part is you will always find the answers.

Chapter Seven

Attract the Wealth you want

"Money is a by-product of your true purpose"

Change the focus, without expectation

Let's face it. Without money, life is challenging. As it is, people have all sorts of problems. There is illness, relationship drama, rebellious children, old parents that are demanding and unsatisfying job. Someone said to me that I motivate him when I talk about attracting wealth but how could he think of attracting wealth when he doesn't have enough money to put fuel into his car to get him to work. He said his priority was to worry about how he will get more money to buy fuel. He went onto say, if he can solve that problem, then he is willing to look into other aspects of his life and attract wealth because at this point, he didn't need wealth, he needed fuel money.

I then kept quiet and smiled at him. He was curious about the silence. I decided to explain something very fundamental to him in a way in which he was able to understand the process and the power of thought.

Firstly, let's dissect his situation, he *complained* about not having money for fuel. He also reinforced his priority of *worrying* about the dilemma he faced and lastly, he was *willing* to consider attracting wealth once his dilemma was resolved.

I asked him if he thought this made any sense and if he could find any good in it. He responded by telling me that it was "all bad".

I went on to explain the following that opened his eyes and not the thoughts in his mind, which exaggerated the reality of the situation:

1. Firstly, he has a job and he should be giving thanks for his job, as there are thousands of people around the world that are hoping and praying for someone to agree to pay them for their services.
2. Secondly, he has a car and should be counting that as a blessing. He may not have fuel money at that moment in time but I am certain that when he gets paid, he has money, he has fuel and his car transports; not just him but his family from point a to b and he does not need to use public transport for his family.

3. If he is able to appreciate and express sincere gratitude for what he has already been blessed with, he would be focusing on the positive and he will see the "problem" as a lot less serious as his mind is making it out to be.
4. There is some limiting belief within him where he believes that he does not deserve money in his life as well as that he lacks self-acceptance and self-love, which is one of the biggest reasons for lack of financial support in one's life.

I then went on to ask him if he ever considered that perhaps the reason he is experiencing lack of the money that he needs for fuel is because he is not conscious of his blessings and neither is he counting them. I suggested that he should try adopting an attitude of gratitude, no matter how "bad" the present moment may seem.

The lesson to be learnt here is that, no matter how bad your situation is, you have nobody to blame but yourself. You cannot blame your employer for not paying you enough; you cannot blame the economy for the price of fuel. You must look within and correct and make changes in order for the outer world to work in your favour.

A simple step like beginning the process of complete self-love and self-acceptance could change your entire life. Let me explain. If you think that you are not good enough – and we all feel that way at some point – you may think that this negative thought would motivate you to achieve more.

Well, that is far from the truth. Once you accept yourself at the deepest level and you let go of the idea that you do not deserve to have anything more than what you do have then that is all you will ever have. If you begin to feel worthy and accept yourself and feel love for your existence, you attract abundance into your life. Do not misunderstand this love and self-acceptance. This should come with modesty and humility, not with pride or arrogance.

*Dhisha used to be a colleague some years back and she would never do a favour for anybody unless there was something she would receive in return for her efforts. Whether it was lending money to a friend, preparing a meal for a social gathering or offering someone a lift home, there was nothing she would do unless there was some sort of gain or benefit for her. She never quite understood the art of giving and receiving. In your life, you must not do anything or make any effort with expectation of something to happen to and for you in return. This action may seem insincere. You must have faith that whatever it is you are doing, you are doing with sincerity and dedication and purpose and then do it. Do not think about the results too much. Do not think about when you will receive your reward. Especially at the time of doing something, remain focused on what you are doing, focus and dedicate your thoughts and your self to it with faith and passion. For example in 2011 I was asked to do an event for a Minister. I was given a 24 hour notice period to pull off a gala cocktail dinner for 200 people which should include food, décor, banners to be designed and printed, technical requirements, guest list, R.S.V.P and everything else that comes with putting an event together. I was introduced to the person who represented the Minister's office and was asked to provide quotes, menu, and centrepiece options the same afternoon. Naturally, I was nervous and the first thought that came to my mind was "Oh, I am so dead!" but then I stopped and said to myself "This is happening to me right now, this is my present moment, I can either make it a success or I can drown in negativity and think about everything that could go wrong". I chose the first option. There was no discussion of my remuneration, any terms and conditions or any detail. Off I went and, within 24 hours, the room was filled with the most beautiful white orchids as centre pieces, branded banners, gorgeous canapés and welcome drinks and the setting was nothing short of perfect. Let's not even elaborate about the fact that I had to run into town at least 3 times that day by foot from the venue of choice, the credit card payment issues, the endless phone calls and the mad rush. But nothing stopped me. I was passionate. I was determined. All negative thoughts were nowhere near my mind. All I kept thinking about was whatever was happening at that moment, so if I was busy with the caterer, my mind was completely in that meeting, completely focused on the food, the menu breakdown and the layout. I was not worried about other outstanding items. Can you understand the importance of embracing the present moment? It means your mind must be free of all other thought that is not associated to whatever is happening in the moment. So I was not thinking about whether I would be getting paid or not, I was not thinking about whether the whether all of my efforts and time would be worth it in the end. I was living in the present moment and dedicating all of my efforts to what was in front of me and being completely grateful for it. Apart from the gala dinner being a success, I was paid double the amount in the end and received an outstanding letter of recommendation from the CEO. The greatest efforts are not concerned with its results.

If you wish to do anything with your life - especially if it involves money - do not focus on your perceived reward. It is when you do not focus on reward that the reward comes to you in abundance. It is out of your sincerity and commitment to assist someone else with a difficulty in their own life, that you will soon receive your own gratification. In order to attract money into your life, you must first understand the process of how money flows.

Money does not flow into anyone's life that does not want money. You must know that millionaires and other wealthy individuals do not necessarily love money but in fact they love the freedom and luxury that the money provides. So by loving what money can provide them with, their mind-set is dedicated to their own self-worth.

Think like an entrepreneur

Millions of people around the world are stuck in jobs that they hate. I mentioned this earlier in the book. They are working because they have to earn an income. It is something where they feel there is no choice. I also spoke to you about self-inspiration and taking action. When you find your true purpose and identify your highest values then it is much easier to follow your path and do something that you love that will bring you money.

So what does thinking like an entrepreneur have to do with anything? Well you see, when you have a mind-set of an entrepreneur, you basically are someone who thinks of more than one way to create income for yourself. You do not limit yourself to one or even two sources of income but in fact you open up your mind to endless possibilities and opportunities for you to create multiple sources of income in your life. However, thinking like an entrepreneur does not just mean finding news ways to make more money, but it involves inspiring other people and helping change their lives at the same time. So you are taking inspired action for yourself and at the same time, you are changing the lives of people around you. Through that, you are changing the world.

Many people do not necessarily know exactly how to derive more than one source of income. Naturally, they would say to themselves, it is already currently so difficult for me to work everyday and earn this salary, where am I going to find time to go out there and find other ways to make money!" Well that is your problem right there! You are right. You will not be able to go out and do anything more than what you are doing is because your mind will not allow you to. Your limiting beliefs will keep you stuck in negativity thinking that you are not able to do more and it will think of all sorts of excuses that you believe and use in your daily talk with others.

If you feel or think or believe that your true purpose is to be an entrepreneur then just know that you are an entrepreneur even before you have taken any action. For the simple fact that you believe that you are capable, you must believe that you possess the quality to be one and you must have the passion and the heart to want to help other people and yourself. Many success stories have come from a man or a woman who complained about something or had an issue that they had to face and it is from that very issue or complaint that a fabulous idea was born! Because they did not ignore that idea, they followed that spark and inspired themselves to act upon it. Soon after, they started a business that became hugely successful that allowed them the freedom that they wanted in their lives. Life will present many opportunities for you to pursue however if you do not become aware of the opportunity that presents itself, you will not be able to pursue it. In order to attract wonderful, amazing new opportunities into your existence, you must change the way you think.

It is easy to say I want to follow my inspiration and do something really great with my life. However, I am going to do this on my own. I don't need anyone to help me; this is going to be my success. I will keep this idea and my inspiration to myself and once I become successful then everyone will get to know about it. Firstly, this is the most dangerous thought that will prove to be detrimental to your success in the future.

If you were put on this earth to live in isolation, what would be the need to be born into a family, what would be the purpose of living with other people or engaging with people right? You would have been born on an island somewhere and interacted with nobody but yourself and life would have been meaningless to you. It is through other people, that we develop and grow. It is through interaction and human engagement that we learn more about ourselves, it is through situations and people that we find inspiration and is able to follow and find our true purpose and pursue our visions. I can understand the belief whereby *Marien was afraid to share her dreams with everyone or boast about what she is still planning to do with fear that she may not do it or that people will call her boastful or having pride as she is talking about something that she has not yet achieved. So there is the fear of failure and embarrassment. However what I am referring to is different. By keeping your visions and goals and ideas to yourself, you are slowing down the process of achieving those goals and visions. It takes people and experiences around you to serve as a stepping-stone towards your own achievements.

So here is a simple suggestion for you. If you wish to start up your own business or you had a great idea that sparked an inspiration and you are now ready to pursue it then why not involve many other people to share your dream with you. A perfect idea would be to contact at least 5 people that you may have worked with or you are friends with whom you think would be able to inspire you and assist you in achieving your vision. And try to list 5 people whom you know also requires help in their own ventures and business ideas. Form a network and meet once a week and see how best each of you could help towards fulfilling your goals and visions. At the following meeting, ask each person to invite 1 other person that they know who could bring their talent and expertise to the network. You will soon have many other people sharing in your vision, introducing you to more people and you may also be able to assist others in their endeavours. So you see what is happening, the more you are able to help others, the more help you will attract into your life. Your success and your achievements will be supported by others, without which you cannot possibly create a successful business. It takes people to make people. But it also takes people who have the interests of others as well as their own at heart to create sustainable income and success. It is only through helping others, that we are able to understand the meaning of entrepreneurship.

If something has inspired a thought in your mind after which you say "hey, I could start a great business with this idea, in fact I am sure I can make great money if I did this!" Then take action. Do not allow the thought to pass and do not see it as "just another thought" or laugh it off.

See it as a sign from your inner self to take inspired action. You may begin with a little research, perhaps conduct a few surveys, speak to people and gauge their interest. This can then be followed by doing some investment homework and write down at least 100 ways in which you think you could actually make that idea a reality. A successful entrepreneur is not someone who tried a few times and got to the top, because his success stemmed from relentless effort to continue to pursue. If one way failed, he believed that there is another possible angle, so long as he believed in all possibilities, it was actually more of an effort to give up. So if you wrote down 100 ways in which you could make that idea a reality, then pursue each one. Do not stop. Pursue. Believe and try again. It is with faith and dedication that the world's most successful entrepreneurs were born from. It is very important to note whether your idea will bring you income and if you think it will, then pursue it. However, try not to think about the money too much, focus and pay more attention to what it is you have a burning passion for, let all of your energy be filled with thoughts and actions on paving way to bring your idea to fruition. The money will come. It must come. I have no doubt that there will be money. The mind-set is more important though.

The Art of Giving

For years, your parents would have stressed upon the importance of charity and giving. Therefore, as children and as we progressed into adulthood, our hearts have opened up towards giving. Perhaps we have learnt how to give away our old clothing, shoes and items that we no longer use. Maybe we give our change to poor people on the roadside or maybe we even decide to feed an orphanage once a month. In whichever way you find suitable, you will give. Generosity is one of the most fundamental virtues in our lives. It is very much a part of all religions and cultures. It is through giving that we are able to receive.

There are many different ways and forms in which we give. Some people give away items, others give money and people even give charity by offering their time to other people. However the giving that I am specifically talking about in this chapter is giving away money and understanding the power that exists within the art of giving money.

For those to prefer to count each and every penny that they earn and keep a strict budget, perhaps included in that budget is the percentage of their income that they choose to contribute towards a needy fund. This is all great and it is definitely the opening of much more abundance in one's life. It is important to understand the flow of money. As explained earlier, money flows through us and not to us. If money flows to you and you do not allow it to flow through and choose to keep it for yourself, you will find yourself not receiving any more.

It is like a door. If I open a door, depending on how wide or narrow I decide to open that door, it is the exact degree to the space I am making for someone to come through that door. If it were a small opening, maybe only one person would be able to enter through that door. The wider I open that door, the more people or things that can come through it. So your money is exactly the same. The more money you give away, is the exact degree to which you will receive money in your life. Many people would use an excuse such as "Well I don't have enough money this month so when I do make enough money then I will feel much more confident about giving it away".

This is my point. You do not need to have a certain amount or reach a certain point of wealth before you decide that it is "safe" to give money away. The best time to ever give money away is when you feel or think that you do not have enough because what you are doing is opening your heart and the door to attract much more of the same into your life. It is as simple as that. And note that you do not need a specific reason to give money away. You can give money away to anyone or any fund that your heart desires. You could help a friend or even a total stranger. You could hear of a charity case that needs financial aid somewhere in the world and make a conscious decision to send them money.

Earlier in the book, I spoke specifically about decoupling yourself from the numbers and emotionally detaching yourself from money. Imagine a world where money belongs to no one. It merely rotates from person to person throughout the world and there is no specific possession of any sort of money.

Likewise, if you have been paid for a job or a good deed, that money does not have your name on it. It has come into your life with a purpose. It will assist you with some sort of luxury or freedom and then it will flow onto the next person. This is the life of money. So of what use is our emotional attachment to money? It needs to be identified and understood for what it is.

In no way must we resent money. If you resent money then you are again, an ungrateful person because it is the very same money that allows you to exchange goods or pay a medical bill. So it should be embraced for the freedom that it provides and then passed onto more people.

Giving is part of existence. When you give, you are generous. It shows that your heart is open to helping other people and improving their lives in some way, even if it is in the smallest way. When you open your heart, it reveals compassion and love for all things created by God. This is direct appreciation to God. Why then, will God and the Universe not bring a flow of abundance back into your life? In fact, the universe will move objects and people and circumstances to bring you abundance for your art of giving.

The one advice I must share with you regarding giving. If you have your last R200.00 on you or even if you have a lot of money on you and for some reason, you are required to pay a bill or give money away, if in your heart, there is a question mark or some sort of hesitation, then do not part with that money. You will be paying that bill or giving away that money half-heartedly and not truly and not from a place of complete trust and faith in God. Therefore, it is safer to keep the money with you. It is when you have a shift in mind-set and your heart becomes open and free and you feel happy to give away that money, must you then part with it. So even if it so happens where you realise and become conscious of yourself and your thoughts where you say "Wow, I have realised that I am not completely happy to be parting with this money and I must first change my intention and thoughts and then give it away"

This is the most enlightening and rewarding thing you could ever do for yourself. When money is given from a place of hesitance and uncertainty, it cannot bring you abundance. In fact, it may bring you a situation in your life where you may experience financial difficulty. So in order to save yourself from such a situation, it is better to become aware of your thoughts and intentions before parting with money, for whatever reason and until you change your mind-set and give that money away from a place of appreciation and joy.

Based on beliefs and manifestation, the world is filled with wealthy people and poor people. If you are wealthy and you enjoy helping others and giving money away because you are fully aware of the abundance that it brings into your life, this is amazing. However, also note that when you choose to help other people, when you choose to increase the abundance in your own life by enhancing the quality of someone else's life, make extra effort in remaining humble in your gestures.

An abundance of blessings lie in the act of giving away money. The most blessed acts from God, the act that is most revered by him, are the ones where one does something without the expectation of reward. To sincerely do something without expectation will bring you closer to God and your true self.

Those are the actions of a modest, humble person, who does not need to be thanked for their actions or receive acclaim for their deeds, for the true art of giving lies in the silence of its efforts.

Once you come to understand that it is best to give money away without anyone else knowing, you will soon understand the sweetness and lightness of being a giver.

So no matter how much you have or even how little you have, if you want to master the art of giving, give it away without expectation of any reward or recognition and in this, you will find the greatest feeling of contentment and inner states of joy. If God has seen it, then God is enough.

Finding Your Purpose – 1

If you are currently working in a job that does not fulfil you, you may want to ask yourself the following questions:

1. How did I end up working in this position for this company?
2. Do I enjoy the tasks that are part of my job description?
3. Do I receive any fulfilment in what I am doing?
4. Am I adding value to this company?
5. Am I prepared to earn this income for the next 5 years of my life?

Based on your answers to the above 5 questions, you will easily identify whether you are working with passion and purpose or you are doing what you are doing simply because it pays the bills at the end of the month.

We all face challenges daily in our life whether it is in our studies, career choice, personal, financial, relationship or health related areas of our lives. However it is important to note that these challenges are the perfect opportunity to create a life of fulfilment and purpose. It is these very challenges that we face, which allow us to identify opportunities and maximise on them.

Each individual has their own set of values and these values have a sliding scale from lowest priority to highest priority. That which is most important to you, you will consider to be your highest value and that which is least important to you, will be considered as a low value.

Let us look at a few examples below:

Example One:

For a typical housewife and mother, her values may be identified below,

Highest Values:

- Taking care of children i.e. preparing meals, transportation, homework & spending quality time with her children
- Household chores i.e. cleaning, washing, dusting and ironing
- Cooking breakfast, lunch and dinner for her family

Lowest Values:

- Getting dressed up and attending social midweek events
- Weekly Hair and make-up appointments
- Joining her spouse for business conferences or dinners

Example Two

A businesswoman who runs a company and a team of 100 staff members,

Highest Values:

- Staff Meetings promptly at 08h00am every morning
- Weekly Hair and make-up appointments
- Employing the most efficient and reliable housekeeper and babysitter

Lowest Values:

- Getting into the kitchen everyday to prepare dinner meals
- Cleaning the house
- Making time to visit family and friends

Based on the above 2 examples, you will easily identify that each woman has her own set of values based on the life that she chose for herself. What may be of utmost importance to one may be irrelevant to the other. This does not mean that one has better higher values than the other.

What needs to be understood is that every individual is unique and is entitled to his or her own set of values.

Now that we understand the difference between highest values and lowest values, it is much easier for you to identify your own set of values. We may change our priorities from time to time and this is perfectly fine. As humans, we evolve, like everything else around us. As time goes by, as circumstances and experiences shift the world around us, so too do our priorities change.

In fact, it is recommended that your values be reviewed every few months so that it gives you a clearer indication of where you are and where your focus is.

Finding your True Purpose and creating your goals

Answer the following questions:

1. What job are you currently working?
2. Do you enjoy your work?
3. What do you enjoy doing that makes you happy?
4. Write down 6 things that you love:

5. List at least 3 things that are energy detractors in your life? You did it because you think you have to but you do not necessarily enjoy doing it as it drains the energy from you.
6. What do you think about the most, most of the time?

Three Steps to creating your success:

1. Create a meaningful goal.

This goal needs to be clearly defined. You need to write down exactly what it is you want to achieve. Be honest to yourself. Look at the things you enjoy doing. What brings a smile to your face? What creates a burning passion within when you engage in it? Once you decide on a meaningful goal, you need to write this down.

What do I see myself doing 5 years from today?

How much money would I be earning 5 years from today?

Describe the lifestyle and the scenario around your life, 5 years from today?

List the top 5 things that you would like to achieve:

Now, re-arrange the above list in accordance to high priority through to lowest priority. What would you like to achieve first.

2. **Plan it with surgical precision!**

For each goal listed above from highest to lowest priority, answer the following questions:

Example:

Goal 1: I want to enrol to study so that I may become a chef

What do I need to do FIRST, which will help me get to my goal?

- I need to save money to pay for my studies.
- I need research possible educational institutions that cover my intended course of study.
- I need to spend more time in the kitchen, experimenting and preparing food.

For each step you outline, you will find that there will be follow-up steps. If you are able to complete one task at a time, you will realise that it is the simple steps that are bringing you closer and closer to your goal. You will be focused on completing the smaller steps, which are also identified as goals as they play a very significant role in directing you towards your goal.

Once you have achieved goal 1, which is enrolment towards studies, you will then set out a second goal and that could be 'I would like to qualify as a chef next year'

Again, you will define 'what do I need to do FIRST which will help me get to my goal'

This cycle will continue until you achieve one goal after the after simply because you remained focus on the smaller, simple steps. In this way, you will not give up easily as you understand that you cannot sit on a couch and say "I want to become a chef" but it is a long process and I don't know where to begin and it is going to take time'

You'll find yourself thinking more than actually doing anything about it. Three years will pass and guess what? You are still thinking. Had you taken action, by identifying the smaller steps that you need to take, you would probably have qualified as a chef by year three and would be getting into a restaurant or hotel as a professional and qualified chef.

This is why it is important for you to understand that success does not happen when you achieve your goal. Success happens when you make a conscious decision to take the first step. Once you take the first step, it is easier for you to walk the path and be guided towards your passion and purpose.

3. <u>Lock the door behind it!</u>

When you have decided on what you goal is. You then create a plan to achieve it. You then lock the door behind it. Which means that no matter what happens, you will not give up. No matter how tough it gets, no matter how many challenges come your way, you will ensure that you continue walking ahead, facing each challenge head on. Embrace them as if they are opportunities for you. Persevere and be determined to overcome your challenges.

If you maintain your ultimate goal in mind and believe that you will achieve it, it will be very easy for you to lock the door behind you and steer ahead!

Should you find yourself in a situation whereby you have reached a crossroad, keep writing down all and any options that you find to work around the path walkers!

For more information on identifying and setting goals and steps to achieving them, you are more than welcome to contact me and I will gladly assist you through this process!

My email address is adila@adivahmarketing.co.za

As long as you believe, then you will achieve!

BONUS FEATURE

Meditation Techniques and their Benefits.

Meditation is a powerful technique that can assist you in reaching a higher level of consciousness as well as self-awareness. Meditation has been in existence for thousands of years and has proved to bring the mind to a place of stillness and calmness. Meditation relaxes the mind and the body and it is food for the soul as well. It allows the humans to look within themselves and involve the mind with a specific purpose. Meditation has proved to be a healing tool for many and it will definitely bring about a sense of being, a sense of peace and serenity. It is something that can be done by any person. You do not need to reach a certain level of spiritually and neither is meditation associated to any specific religious belief. It is something that can be practised by any individual that seeks to still the mind and silence the chatter of the brain.

When one meditates, they are engaging in a very natural activity as they become one with themselves. You actually freeze your existence in your external world and begin to focus and pay more attention to your inner world. You are giving more attention to your soul and you are awakening a level of consciousness within you. You become more observant and much more calm at the same time. Whilst in a state of meditation, you may find yourself free of all thought however your predominant thought would be of God and your love for God.

Meditation brings about positivity in your mind and in your entire existence. Your quality of life will improve as you spend more time with yourself. You may even find that your sleeping patterns will become much more regular, your health will improve and you will be less anxious and more calm in situations that arise in your daily life. You will also find yourself handling situations in a much better manner as your mind is well balanced and is able to think much more clearly before you take an action.

You do not have to sit in any particular position although there is several recommended sitting positions for meditation. It is, however, important to be seated or even lying down in a position that is comfortable and bearable for you. Many people choose to meditate on a prayer mat or in a place where they offer their daily prayer to God. This is perfectly fine as it is the place where you feel most connected to your Creator.

In order to connect with the consciousness of your mind, breathing techniques are very important.

Your breathing must be consistent and include deep inhalation but breath in slowly feeling and hearing every moment of that inhalation. You will feel your lungs expanding as you breath in. Choose to become aware and completely conscious of everything that is happening in your mind. You will then hold your breath for a few seconds and then exhale, again slowly through your mouth. Be aware of your exhalation. Be aware of your lungs contracting and consistently continue this breathing exercise throughout your meditation session.

Many people have specific prayers, praise to God and even affirmations that they wish to verbalise during the process of meditation. Another recommended form of meditation is facing one's face and chin downward towards the heart, the left side of your chest, closing your eyes and sending praise to God whilst breathing in and out slowly. You may also want to visualise the name God written on your heart and picture a beautiful colour of gold and shimmer emanate from your heart as you see God's name beat each time as your heart beats. You may also practise your breathing according to your heartbeat and for each breath you take in and let out, you will see God's name.

About The Author

Adila Vahed is a 27-year-old entrepreneur who has inspired the young and the old in her life.

She comes from a family of 4 sisters and is the eldest sibling. From young, Adila was always interested in reading and writing and English was her most enjoyed subject at school.

She never really knew what she wanted to do when she completed school. Her journey started with studies in hotel management, travel & tourism and even journalism. Whilst studying, Adila decided to volunteer her services to the hotel & travel industry to gain experience. Her voluntary work, however, extended far beyond this industry and she enjoyed offering her services to a local community radio station, a Halaal authority organisation, hotels & even a travel agency. Her work experience allowed her to pursue employment within the hotel industry where she began as a receptionist for a popular hotel on Durban's beachfront and worked her way through to sales and marketing management in a few other hotel groups.

Having spent almost 9 years within the tourism and hospitality industry, Adila Vahed opened Adivah In Africa Pty Ltd in September 2011. Her company specialises in strategic hotel marketing, conference & Event Management as well as providing inspirational workshops to her clients and their staff.

Adila is a professional & efficient conference and event manager and offers strategic marketing programmes to the hospitality industry however her passion for people along with her own personal life experiences inspired the birth of "Get out of Your Mind!"

Adila has searched for answers to many questions over the years in pursuit of understanding the mind of an individual and how we have become victims of it. Through research and dedication, this book was given life.

Adila is inspired to awaken the minds of other young entrepreneur's, students and people from all walks of life. She is a young entrepreneur and a mother and firmly believes that being authentic and original has been the best thing she has ever done for herself

For more information on the Get out of Your Mind! Inspirational Workshops, visit the following websites:

www.GetoutofyourMind.com or visit www.adivah.co.za

Made in the USA
Coppell, TX
04 January 2023

10411760R00105